Materialism
and the
Dialectical
Method

By MAURICE CORNFORTH

D1246397

INTERNATIONAL PUBLISHERS, NEW YORK

In Memory of David Guest

Volume One of the 3-volume
Dialectical Materialism: An Introduction

SBN 7178-0326-0

Printed in the United States of America

CONTENTS

AUTHOR'S NOTE ON
THE FOURTH EDITION

This little book on Materialism and the Dialectical Method originated from lectures given under the auspices of the London District Committee of the Communist Party of Great Britain in 1950. That was a long time ago and a lot has been thought and written on the subject since then. I am glad that nevertheless it has continued to be found useful—though to try to make it so I have now had to revise it three times over.

In these revisions I have changed as little as possible. In preparing this fourth edition I have made mostly only minor stylistic changes intended to render the meaning clearer and avoid misunderstandings. In particular I have left intact references to J. V. Stalin's booklet on *Dialectical and Historical Materialism* and Mao Tse-tung's lecture *On Contradictions*, both of which seem to me to remain worthy of quotation whatever may be objected against other words and deeds of their authors. The only substantial change I have made is in the reference to biology and the controversial theories of Trofim Lysenko in Chapter 7, where what I had written originally was obviously written in error.

I would like to stress that this book has no pretentions to be anything more than "an Introduction". It is not a textbook of Marxist philosophy but an introduction to some key philosophical ideas of Marxism which it still remains for Marxists to work out, criticise and develop further.

M.C.
London, January 1968

PART ONE
MATERIALISM

Chapter One

PARTY PHILOSOPHY

Party Philosophy and Class Philosophy

A revolutionary working-class party needs a revolutionary working-class philosophy, and that philosophy is dialectical materialism.

This assertion may appear a strange one, both to many politicians and to many philosophers. But we will not begin to understand dialectical materialism unless we can grasp the thought which lies behind it.

Let us ask, first of all, what conception of philosophy lies behind the assertion that a political party or—since a party is always the political representative of a class—a class needs to work out and adopt a definite philosophy of its own.

By philosophy is usually meant our most general account of the nature of the world and of mankind's place and destiny in it—our world outlook.

That being understood, it is evident that everybody has some kind of philosophy, even though he has never learned to discuss it. Everybody is influenced by philosophical views, even though he has not thought them out for himself and cannot formulate them.

Some people, for example, think that this world is nothing but "a vale of tears" and that our life in it is the preparation for a better life in another and better world. They accordingly believe that we should suffer whatever befalls us with fortitude, not struggling against it, but trying to do whatever good we can to our fellow creatures. This is one kind of philosophy, one kind of world outlook.

Other people think that the world is a place to grow rich in,

7

and that each should look out for himself. This is another kind of philosophy.

But granted that our philosophy is our world outlook, the task arises of working out this world outlook systematically and in detail, turning it into a well-formulated and coherent theory, turning vaguely held popular beliefs and attitudes into more or less systematic doctrines. This is what the philosophers do.

By the time the philosophers have worked out their theories, they have often produced something very complicated, very abstract and very hard to understand. But even though only a comparatively few people may read and digest the actual productions of philosophers, these productions may and do have a very wide influence. For the fact that philosophers have systematised certain beliefs reinforces those beliefs, and helps to impose them upon wide masses of ordinary people. Hence, everyone is influenced in one way or another by philosophers, even though they have never read the works of those philosophers.

And if this is the case, then we cannot regard the systems of the philosophers as being wholly products of the brain-work of the individual philosophers. Of course, the formulation of views, the peculiar ways in which they are worked out and written down, is the work of the particular philosopher. But the views themselves, in their most general aspect, have a social basis in ideas which reflect the social activities and social relations of the time, and which, therefore, do not spring ready-made out of the heads of philosophers.

From this we may proceed a step further.

When society is divided into classes—and society always has been divided into classes ever since the dissolution of the primitive communes, that is to say, throughout the entire historical period to which the history of philosophy belongs—then the various views which are current in society always express the outlooks of various classes. We may conclude, therefore, that the various systems of the philosophers also always express a class outlook. They are, in fact, nothing but the systematic working out and theoretical formulation of a

8

class outlook, or, if you prefer, of the ideology of definite classes.

Philosophy is and always has been class philosophy. Philosophers may not realise this, but that does not alter the fact.

For people do not and cannot think in isolation from society, and therefore from the class interests and class struggles which pervade society, any more than they can live and act in such isolation. A philosophy is a world outlook, an attempt to understand the world, mankind and man's place in the world. Such an outlook cannot be anything but the outlook of a class, and the philosopher functions as the thinking representative of a class. How can it be otherwise? Philosophies are not imported from some other planet, but are produced here on earth, by people involved, whether they like it or not, in existing class relations and class struggles. Therefore, whatever philosophers say about themselves, there is no philosophy which does not embody a class outlook, or which is impartial, as opposed to partisan, in relation to class struggles. Search as we may, we shall not find any impartial, non-partisan, non-class philosophy.

Bearing this in mind, then, we shall find that the philosophies of the past have all, in one way or another, expressed the outlook of the so-called "educated" classes, that is to say, of the exploiting classes. In general, it is the leaders of society who express and propagate their ideas in the form of systematic philosophies. And up to the appearance of the modern working class, which is the peculiar product of capitalism, these leaders have always been the exploiting classes. It is their outlook which has dominated philosophy, just as they have dominated society.

We can only conclude from this that the working class, if today it intends to take over leadership of society, needs to express its own class outlook in philosophical form, and to oppose this philosophy to the philosophies which express the outlook and defend the interests of the exploiters.

"The services rendered by Marx and Engels to the working class may be expressed in a few words thus: they taught the working class to know itself and be conscious of itself, and they substituted science for dreams," wrote Lenin in his obituary on Fredrick Engels. Marx and Engels founded and established the revolutionary theory of working-class struggle, which illumines the road by which the working class can throw off capitalist exploitation, can take the leadership of all the masses of the people, and so free the whole of society once and for all of all oppression and exploitation of man by man. They taught that without its own party, independent of all bourgeois parties, the working class certainly could not win victory over capitalism, could not lead the whole of society forward to the abolition of capitalism and the establishment of socialism. Lenin further developed the Marxist teachings about the party. He showed that the party must act as the vanguard of its class, the most conscious section of its class, and that it is the instrument for winning and wielding political power.

To fulfil such a rôle, the party must evidently have knowledge, understanding and vision; in other words, it must be equipped with revolutionary theory, on which its policies are based and by which its activities are guided.

This theory is the theory of Marxism. And it is not just an economic theory, nor yet exclusively a political theory, but a world outlook—a philosophy. Economic and political views are not and never can be independent of a general world outlook. Specific economic and political views express the world outlook of those who hold such views, and conversely, philosophical views find expression in views on economics and politics.

Recognising all this, a revolutionary party of the working class cannot but formulate, and having formulated, hold fast to, develop and treasure, its party philosophy. In this philosophy—dialectical materialism—are embodied the general ideas by means of which the party understands the world which it is seeking to change and in terms of which it defines its aims and works out how to fight for them. In this philosophy are embodied the general ideas by means of which the party seeks to enlighten and organise the whole class, and to influence, guide and win over all the masses of working people, showing the conclusions which must be drawn from each stage of the struggle, helping people to learn from their own experience how to go forward towards socialism.

And so we see why it is that in our times a philosophy has arisen which expresses the revolutionary world outlook of the working class.

Experience itself has taught the party the need for philosophy. For experience shows that if we do not have our own revolutionary socialist philosophy, then inevitably we borrow our ideas from hostile, anti-socialist sources. If we do not adopt today the outlook of the working class and of the struggle for socialism, then we adopt—or slip into, without meaning to do so—that of the capitalists and of the struggle against socialism. This is why the working-class party—if it is to be the genuine revolutionary leadership of its class, and is not to mislead its class by the importation of hostile capitalist ideas, and of policies corresponding to such ideas—must be concerned to formulate, defend and propagate its own revolutionary philosophy.

Class Philosophy and Truth

Against what has just been said about a class and party philosophy, the objection is bound to be raised that such a conception is a complete travesty of the whole idea of philosophy.

Class interests may incline us to believe one thing rather than another, some will say, but should not philosophy be above this? Should not philosophy be objective and impartial, and teach us to set class and party interests aside, and to seek only for the truth? For surely what is true is true, whether this suits some or other class interests or not? If philosophy is partisan— party philosophy—how can it be objective, how can it be true philosophy?

In reply to such objections, we may say that the working-class standpoint in philosophy is very far indeed from having no concern for truth.

Is there no such thing as truth? Of course there is—and

men are getting nearer to it. For different outlooks, partisan as they may be, are not on a level so far as nearness to truth is concerned. Every philosophy embodies a class outlook. Yes, but just as one class differs from another class in its social rôle and in its contribution to the development of society, so one philosophy embodies positive achievements in comparison with another in the working out of the truth about the world and society.

People are prone to believe that if we adopt a partisan, class standpoint, then we turn our backs on truth; and that, on the other hand, if we genuinely seek for truth, then we must be strictly impartial and non-partisan. But the contrary is the case. It is only when we adopt the partisan standpoint of historically the most progressive class that we are able to get nearer to truth.

The definition of dialectical materialism, therefore, as the philosophy of the revolutionary working-class party, is in no way incompatible with the claim of dialectical materialism to express truth, and to be a means of arriving at truth. On the contrary. We have every right to make this claim, in view of the actual historical position and rôle of the working class.

Except for the working class, all other classes which have aspired to take the leadership of society have been exploiting classes. But every exploiting class, whatever its achievements, has always to find some way of *disguising* its real position and aims, both from itself and from the exploited, and of making out that its rule is just and permanent. For such a class can never recognise its real position and aims as an exploiting class, or the temporary character of its own system.

For example, in ancient slave society, Aristotle, the greatest philosopher of antiquity, made out that the institution of slavery was decreed by nature, since some men were by nature slaves.

In the heyday of feudal society the greatest philosopher of the middle ages, Thomas Aquinas, represented the entire universe as being a kind of feudal system. Everything was arranged in a feudal hierarchy, with God surrounded by the chief archangels at the top. Everything depended on what was next above it in the system, and nothing could exist without God.

As for capitalism, it dissolves all feudal ties and, as Marx and Engels observed in *The Communist Manifesto*, "has left remaining no other nexus between man and man than naked self-interest, than callous cash payment". This was reflected in the beginnings of capitalist philosophy, especially in Britain.

This philosophy saw the world as consisting of independent atoms, each complete in itself, concerned only with itself, and all interacting. This was a mirror of capitalist society, as seen by the rising bourgeoisie. And by means of such ideas they succeeded, too, in disguising their own aims of domination and profit. Worker and capitalist were "on a level", each was a free human atom, and they entered into a free contract, the one to work, the other to provide capital and pay wages.

But the working class does not need any such "false consciousness" as is contained in such philosophies. It does not want to set up a new system of exploitation, but to abolish all exploitation of man by man. For this reason, it has no interest whatever in disguising anything, but rather in understanding things just as they really are. For the better it understands the truth, the more is it strengthened in its struggle.

Moreover, other classes have always wanted to perpetuate themselves and to last out for as long as they could. And so they have favoured philosophical "systems" which give themselves a permanent place in the universe. Such systems attempt to define the nature of the universe so as to represent certain things and certain relations as being necessary, eternal and unchangeable. And then they make it appear that a particular social system is a necessary part of the whole.

But the working class does not need to perpetuate itself. On the contrary, it needs to do away with its own existence as a class as quickly as possible, and to establish a classless society. Therefore, the working class has no use at all for any philosophical "system" which establishes any false permanence. Its class position and aims are such that it can afford to and needs to recognise and trace out the change, coming into being and ceasing to be of *everything* in existence.

Our party philosophy, then, has a right to lay claim to truth. For it is the only philosophy which is based on a standpoint which demands that we should always seek to understand things just as they are, in all their manifold changes and interconnections, without disguises and without fantasy.

A Revolution in Philosophy

"The Marxian doctrine is omnipotent because it is true," wrote Lenin. "It is complete and harmonious, and provides men with an integral world conception which is irreconcilable with any form of superstition, reaction or defence of bourgeois oppression" (*The Three Sources and Three Component Parts of Marxism*).

And he further wrote:

"There is nothing resembling 'sectarianism' in Marxism, in the sense of its being a hidebound, petrified doctrine, a doctrine which arose *away from* the highroad of development of world civilisation. On the contrary, the genius of Marx consists precisely in the fact that he furnished answers to questions the foremost minds of mankind had already raised. His teachings arose as the direct and immediate *continuation* of the teachings of the greatest representatives of philosophy, political economy and socialism. . . ."

In its philosophical aspect, Marxism appears as the culmination of a whole great development of philosophical thought, in which the problems of philosophy were posed and took shape in the course of a series of revolutions, its highest point being reached in the classical German philosophy of the early nineteenth century.

But if Marxism is thus the continuation and culmination of the past achievements of philosophy, it is a continuation which puts an end to an epoch and constitutes a new point of departure. For in comparison with past philosophies, it launches out on new lines. It constitutes a revolution in philosophy, an end to the "systems" of the past, a philosophy of an entirely new kind.

Marxism is no longer a philosophy which expresses the world outlook of an exploiting class, of a minority, striving

14

to impose its rule and its ideas upon the masses of the people, in order to keep them in subjection; but it is a philosophy which serves the common people in their struggle to throw off all exploitation and to build a classless society.

Marxism is a philosophy which seeks to understand the world in order to change it. "The philosophers have only interpreted the world in various ways," wrote Marx. "The point, however, is to change it." Therefore, if we could say of past philosophy that it has been an attempt to understand the world and man's place and destiny in it—an attempt necessarily conditioned by the class outlook, prejudices and illusions of the various exploiting class philosophers—we have to say of Marxist philosophy that it is an attempt to understand the world in order to change the world and to shape and realise man's destiny in it. Dialectical materialism is a theoretical instrument in the hands of the people for use in changing the world.

Marxism, therefore, seeks to base our ideas of things on nothing but the actual investigation of them, arising from and tested by experience and practice. It does not invent a "system" as previous philosophies have done, and then try to make everything fit into it.

Thus dialectical materialism is in the truest sense a popular philosophy, a scientific philosophy and a philosophy of practice.

The revolutionary characteristics of dialectical materialism are embodied in the two features of Marxist philosophy which give it its name—dialectics and materialism.

In order to understand things so as to change them we must study them, not according to the dictates of any abstract system, but in their real changes and interconnections—and that is what is meant by dialectics.

We must set aside preconceived ideas and fancies about things, and strive to make our theories correspond to the real conditions of material existence—and that means that our outlook and theory is materialistic.

In dialectical materialism, wrote Engels, in his book *Ludwig Feuerbach*, "the materialist world outlook was taken really seriously for the first time and was carried through consistently. . . ." For "it was resolved to comprehend the real world—nature and history—just as it presents itself to everyone who approaches it free from preconceived idealist fancies. It was decided relentlessly to sacrifice every idealist fancy which could not be brought into harmony with the facts conceived in their own and not in a fantastic connection. And materialism means nothing more than this."

Chapter Two

MATERIALISM AND IDEALISM

Materialism and Idealism—Opposed Ways of Interpreting Every Question

Materialism is not a dogmatic system. It is rather a way of interpreting, conceiving of, explaining every question.

The materialist way of interpreting events, of conceiving of things and their interconnections, is opposed to the idealist way of interpreting and conceiving of them. Materialism is opposed to idealism. On every question, there are materialist and idealist ways of interpreting it, materialist and idealist ways of trying to understand it.

Thus materialism and idealism are not two opposed abstract theories about the nature of the world, of small concern to ordinary practical folk. They are opposed ways of interpreting and understanding every question, and, consequently, they express opposite approaches in practice and lead to very different conclusions in terms of practical activity.

Nor are they, as some use the terms, opposite moral attitudes —the one high-minded, the other base and self-seeking. If we use the terms like this, we will never understand the opposition between idealist and materialist conceptions; for this way of speaking is, as Engels said, nothing but

"an unpardonable concession to the traditional philistine prejudice against the word materialism resulting from the long-continued defamation by the priests. By the word materialism the philistine understands gluttony, drunken-ness, lust of the eye, lust of the flesh, arrogance, cupidity, miserliness, profit-hunting and stock-exchange swindling—

in short, all the filthy vices in which he himself indulges in private. By the word idealism he understands the belief in virtue, universal philanthropy and in a general way a 'better world', of which he boasts before others" (*Ludwig Feuerbach*).

Before trying to define materialism and idealism in general terms, let us consider how these two ways of understanding things are expressed in relation to certain simple and familiar questions. This will help us to grasp the significance of the distinction between a materialist and an idealist interpretation.

First let us consider a very familiar natural phenomenon—a thunderstorm. What causes thunderstorms?

An idealist way of answering this question is to say that thunderstorms are due to the anger of God. Being angry, he arranges for lightning and thunderbolts to descend upon mankind.

The materialist way of understanding thunderstorms is opposed to this. The materialist will try to explain and understand thunderstorms as being solely due to what we call natural forces. For example, ancient materialists suggested that far from thunderstorms being due to the anger of the gods, they were caused by material particles in the clouds banging against one another. That this particular explanation was wrong, is not the point: the point is that it was an attempt at materialist as opposed to idealist explanation. Nowadays a great deal more is known about thunderstorms arising from the scientific investigation of the natural forces involved. Knowledge remains very incomplete, but at all events enough is known to make it quite clear that the explanation must be on materialist lines, so that the idealist explanation has become thoroughly discredited.

It will be seen that while the idealist explanation tries to relate the phenomenon to be explained to some *spiritual* cause—in this case the anger of God—the materialist explanation relates it to *material* causes.

In this example, most educated people today would agree in accepting the materialist interpretation. This is because they generally accept the *scientific* explanation of natural phenomena, and every advance of natural science is an advance in the *materialist* understanding of nature.

Let us take a second example, this time one arising out of social life. For instance: Why are there rich and poor? This is a question which many people ask, especially poor people.

The most straightforward idealist answer to this question is to say simply—it is because God made them so. It is the will of God that some should be rich and others poor.

But other less straightforward idealist explanations are more in vogue. For example: it is because some men are careful and farsighted, and these husband their resources and grow rich, while others are thriftless and stupid, and these remain poor. Those who favour this type of explanation say that it is all due to eternal "human nature". The nature of man and of society is such that the distinction of rich and poor necessarily arises.

Just as in the case of the thunderstorm, so in the case of the rich and poor, the idealist seeks for some spiritual cause—if not in the will of God, the divine mind, then in certain innate characteristics of the human mind.

The materialist, on the other hand, seeks the reason in the material, economic conditions of social life. If society is divided into rich and poor, it is because the production of the material means of life is so ordered that some have possession of the land and other means of production while the rest have to work for them. However hard they may work and however much they may scrape and save, the non-possessors will remain poor, while the possessors grow rich on the fruits of their labour.

On such questions, therefore, the difference between a materialist and an idealist conception can be very important. And the difference is important not merely in a theoretical but in a practical sense.

A materialist conception of thunderstorms, for example, helps us to take precautions against them, such as fitting buildings with lightning conductors. But if our explanation of thunderstorms is idealist, all we can do is to watch and pray. If we accept an idealist account of the existence of rich and poor, all we can do is to accept the existing state of affairs—rejoicing in our superior status and bestowing a little charity if we are rich, and cursing our fate if we are poor. But armed with a materialist understanding of society we can begin to see the way to change society.

It is clear, therefore, that while some may have a vested interest in idealism, it is in the interests of the great majority to learn to think and to understand things in the materialist way.

How, then, can we define materialism and idealism, and the difference between them, in general terms, so as to define the essence of the question? This was done by Engels in the book on *Ludwig Feuerbach.*

> "The great basic question of all philosophy, especially of modern philosophy, is that concerning the relation of thinking and being. . . . The answers which the philosophers have given to this question split them into two great camps. Those who asserted the primacy of spirit to nature and therefore in the last instance assumed world creation in some form or another . . . comprised the camp of idealism. The others, who regarded nature as primary, belong to the various schools of materialism."

Idealism is the way of interpreting things which regards the spiritual as prior to the material, whereas materialism regards the material as prior. Idealism supposes that everything material is dependent on and determined by something spiritual, whereas materialism recognises that everything spiritual is dependent on and determined by something material. And this difference manifests itself both in general philosophical conceptions of the world as a whole, and in conceptions of particular things and events.

Idealism and the Supernatural

At bottom, idealism is religion, theology. "Idealism is clericalism," wrote Lenin in his *Philosophical Notebooks.* All idealism is a continuation of the religious approach to questions, even though particular idealist theories have shed their religious skin. Idealism is inseparable from superstition, belief in the supernatural, the mysterious and unknowable.

Materialism, on the other hand, seeks for explanations in terms belonging to the material world, in terms of factors which we can verify, understand and control.

The roots of the idealist conception of things are, then, the same as those of religion.

To believers, the conceptions of religion, that is to say, conceptions of supernatural spiritual beings, generally seem to have their justification, not, of course, in any evidence of the senses, but in something which lies deep within the spiritual nature of man. And, indeed, it is true that these conceptions do have very deep roots in the historical development of human consciousness. But what is their origin, how did such conceptions arise in the first place? We can certainly not regard such conceptions as being the products, as religion itself tells us, of divine revelation, or as arising from any other supernatural cause, if we find that they themselves have a natural origin. And such an origin can in fact be traced.

Conceptions of the supernatural, and religious ideas in general, owe their origin first of all to the helplessness and ignorance of men in face of the forces of nature. Forces which men cannot understand are personified—they are represented as manifestations of the activity of spirits.

For example, such alarming events as thunderstorms were, as we have seen, explained fantastically as due to the anger of gods. Again, such important phenomena as the growth of crops were put down to the activity of a spirit: it was believed that it was the corn spirit that made the corn grow.

From the most primitive times men personified natural forces in this way. With the birth of class society, when men were impelled to act by social relations which dominated them and which they did not understand, they further invented supernatural agencies doubling, as it were, the state of society. The gods were invented superior to mankind, just as the kings and lords were superior to the common people.

All religion, and all idealism, has at its heart this kind of *doubling of the world*. It is dualistic, and invents a dominating ideal or supernatural world over against the real material world.

Very characteristic of idealism are such antitheses as: soul and body; god and man; the heavenly kingdom and the earthly kingdom; the forms and ideas of things, grasped by the intellect, and the world of material reality, perceptible by the senses.

For idealism, there is always a higher, more real, non-material world—which is prior to the material world, is its ultimate source and cause, and to which the material world is subject. For materialism, on the other hand, there is *one* world, the material world.

By idealism in philosophy we mean any doctrine which says that beyond material reality there is a higher, spiritual reality, in terms of which the material reality is in the last analysis to be explained.

Some Varieties of Present-day Idealist Philosophy

At this point a few observations may be useful concerning some characteristic doctrines of modern bourgeois philosophy.

For nearly three hundred years there has been put forward a variety of philosophy known as "subjective idealism". This teaches that the material world does not exist at all. Nothing exists but the sensations and ideas in our minds, and there is no external material reality corresponding to them.

And then again, this subjective idealism is put forward in the form of a doctrine concerning knowledge: it denies that we can know anything about objective reality outside ourselves, and says that we can have knowledge of appearances only and not of "things in themselves".

This sort of idealism has become very fashionable today. It even parades as extremely "scientific". When capitalism was still a progressive force, bourgeois thinkers used to believe that we could know more and more about the real world, and so control natural forces and improve the lot of mankind indefinitely. Now they are saying that the real world is unknowable, the arena of mysterious forces which pass our comprehension.

We have seen that, at bottom, idealism always believes in *two worlds*, the ideal and the material, and it places the ideal prior to and above the material. Materialism, on the other hand, knows one world only, the material world, and refuses to invent a second, imaginary, superior ideal world.

Materialism and idealism are irreconcilably opposed. But this does not stop many philosophers from trying to reconcile and combine them. In philosophy there are also various attempted compromises between idealism and materialism.

One such attempted compromise is often known as "dualism". Such a compromise philosophy asserts the existence of the spiritual as separate and distinct from the material—but it tries to place the two on a level. Thus it treats the world of non-living matter in a thoroughly materialist way: this, it says, is the sphere of activity of natural forces, and spiritual factors do not enter into it and have nothing to do with it in any way. But when it comes to mind and society, here, says this philosophy, is the sphere of activity of spirit. Here, it maintains, we must seek explanations in idealist and not in materialist terms.

Such a compromise between materialism and idealism, therefore, amounts to this—that with regard to all the most important questions concerning men, society and history we are to continue to adopt idealist conceptions and to oppose materialism.

Another compromise philosophy is known as "realism". In its modern form, this philosophy has arisen in opposition to subjective idealism.

The "realist" philosophers say that the external material world really exists independent of our perceptions and is in some way reflected by our perceptions. In this the "realists" agree with the materialists in opposition to *subjective* idealism; indeed, you cannot be a materialist unless you are a thoroughgoing realist on the question of the real existence of the material world.

But merely to assert that the external world exists independent of our perceiving it, is not to be a materialist. For example, the great Catholic philosopher of the middle ages, Thomas

Aquinas, was in this sense a "realist". And to this day most Catholic theologians regard it as a heresy to be anything but a "realist" in philosophy. But at the same time they assert that the material world, which really exists, was created by God, and is sustained and ruled all the time by the power of God, by a spiritual power. So far from being materialists, they are idealists.

Moreover, the word "realism" is much abused by philosophers. So long as you believe that something or other is "real", you may call yourself a "realist". Some philosophers think that not only is the world of material things real, but that there is also, outside space and time, a real world of "universals", of the abstract essences of things: so these call themselves "realists". Others say that, although nothing exists but the perceptions in our minds, nevertheless these perceptions are real: so these call themselves "realists" too. All of which goes to show that some philosophers are very tricky in their use of words.

The Basic Teachings of Materialism in Opposition to Idealism
In opposition to all the forms of idealism, and of tricky compromises between materialism and idealism, the basic teachings of materialism can be formulated very simply and clearly.

To grasp the essence of these teachings we should also understand what are the main assertions made in every form of idealism. There are three such main assertions of idealism.

1. Idealism asserts that the material world is dependent on the spiritual.
2. Idealism asserts that spirit, or mind, or idea, can and does exist in separation from matter. (The most extreme form of this assertion is subjective idealism, which asserts that matter does not exist at all but is pure illusion.)
3. Idealism asserts that there exists a realm of the mysterious and unknowable, "above", or "beyond", or "behind" what can be ascertained and known by perception, experience and science.

The basic teachings of materialism stand in opposition to these three assertions of idealism.

1. Materialism teaches that the world is by its very nature material, that everything which exists comes into being on the basis of material causes, arises and develops in accordance with the laws of motion of matter.
2. Materialism teaches that matter is objective reality existing outside and independent of the mind; and that far from the mental existing in separation from the material, everything mental or spiritual is a product of material processes.
3. Materialism teaches that the world and its laws are knowable, and that while much in the material world may not be known there is no unknowable sphere of reality which lies outside the material world.

The Marxist philosophy is characterised by its absolutely consistent materialism all along the line, by its making no concessions whatever at any point to idealism.

Materialism and Idealism in Practice

As was pointed out above, the opposition of materialism and idealism—which has now been stated in its most general terms—is not an opposition between abstract theories of the nature of the world, but is an opposition between different ways of understanding and interpreting every question. That is why it is of such profound importance.

Let us consider some of the very practical ways in which the opposition of materialism and idealism is manifested.

Idealists tell us, for example, not to place "too much" reliance on science. They tell us that the most important truths are beyond the reach of science. Hence they encourage us not to believe things on the basis of evidence, experience, practice, but to take them on trust from those who pretend to know best and to have some "higher" source of information.

In this way idealism is a very good friend and standby of every form of reactionary propaganda. It is the philosophy of the capitalist press and the B.B.C. It favours superstitions of all sorts, prevents us from thinking for ourselves and making a scientific approach to moral and social problems.

Again, idealists tell us that what is most important for us all is the inner life of the soul. They tell us that we shall never solve our human problems except by some inner regeneration. This is a favourite theme in the speeches of well-fed persons. But many workers fall for it too—in factories, for example, where a "Moral Rearmament" group is active. They tell you not to fight for better conditions, but to improve your soul. They do not tell you that the best way to improve yourself both materially and morally is to join in the fight for peace and socialism.

Again, an idealist approach is common amongst many socialists. Many sincere socialists, for example, think that what is essentially wrong with capitalism is that goods are unfairly distributed, and that if only we could get everyone, including the capitalists, to accept a new conception of fairness and justice, then we could do away with the evils of capitalism. Socialism to them is nothing but the realisation of an abstract idea of justice.

The idealism of this belief lies in its assumption that it is simply the *ideas* which we hold that determine the way we live and the way society is organised. Those who think in this way forget to look for the *material* causes. For what in fact determines the way goods are distributed in capitalist society —the wealth enjoyed by one part of society, while the other and greater part lives in poverty—is not the ideas which men hold about the distribution of wealth, but the material fact that the mode of production rests on the exploitation of the worker by the capitalist. So long as this mode of production remains in existence, so long will extremes of wealth and poverty remain, and so long will socialist ideas of justice be opposed by capitalist ideas of justice. The task of socialists, therefore, is to organise and lead the struggle of the working class against the capitalist class to the point where the working class takes power from the capitalist class.

If we do not understand this, then we cannot find the way to fight effectively for socialism. We shall find that our socialist ideals are constantly disappointed and betrayed. Such, indeed, has been the experience of British socialism.

It can be seen from these examples how idealism serves as a weapon of reaction; and how when socialists embrace idealism they are being influenced by the ideology of the capitalists. We can no more take over and use capitalist ideas for the purposes of socialist theory than we can take over and use the capitalist state machine, with all its institutions and officials, for the purposes of building socialism.

Right through history, indeed, idealism has been a weapon of reaction. Whatever fine systems of philosophy have been invented, idealism has been used as a means of justifying the rule of an exploiting class and deceiving the exploited.

This is not to say that truths have not been expressed in an idealist guise. Of course they have. For idealism has very deep roots in our ways of thinking, and so men often clothe their thoughts and aspirations in idealist dress. But the idealist form is always an impediment, a hindrance in the expression of truth—a source of confusion and error.

Again, progressive movements in the past have adopted and fought under an idealist ideology. But this has shown only that they contained in themselves the seeds of future reaction—inasmuch as they represented the striving of a new exploiting class to come to power; or that they were themselves influenced by ideas of reaction; or it has been a mark of their weakness and immaturity.

For example, the great revolutionary movement of the English bourgeoisie in the seventeenth century fought under idealist, religious slogans. But the same appeal to God which justified Cromwell in the execution of the King justified him also in stamping out the Levellers.

Early democrats and socialists had many idealist notions. But in their case this demonstrated the *immaturity* and *weakness* of the movement. The idealist illusions had to be overcome if the revolutionary working-class movement was to arise and triumph. As the movement grew strong, the continuance within it of idealist notions represented an alien, reactionary influence.

We can truly say that idealism is essentially a conservative force—an ideology helping the defence of things as they are,

27

and the preservation of illusions in men's minds about their true condition.

On the other hand, every real social advance—every increase in the productive forces, every advance of science—generates materialism and is helped along by materialist ideas. And the whole history of human thought has been the history of the fight of materialism against idealism, of the overcoming of idealist illusions and fantasies.

Materialism teaches us to have confidence in ourselves, in the working class—in people. It teaches us that there are no mysteries beyond our understanding, that we need not accept that which is as being the will of God, that we should contemptuously reject the "authoritative" teachings of those who set up to be our masters, and that we can ourselves understand nature and society so as to be able to change them.

Chapter Three

MECHANISTIC MATERIALISM

The Changing World and How to Understand It
Before Marx, materialism was predominantly *mechanistic.*

We often hear people complain that the materialists seek to reduce everything in the world, including life and mind, to a system of soulless mechanism, to a mere mechanical interaction of bodies. This refers to mechanistic materialism. Marxist materialism is, however, not mechanistic but dialectical. To understand what this means we need first to understand something about mechanistic materialism itself.

We can approach this problem by asking how materialists have sought to understand the various processes of change which are observed everywhere in the world.

The world is full of change. Night follows day and day night; the seasons succeed each other; people are born, grow old and die. Every philosophy recognises that change is an omnipresent fact. The question is: how are we to understand the change which we observe everywhere?

Change may be understood, in the first place, in an idealist way or in a materialist way.

Idealism traces back all change to some idea or intention— if not human, then divine. Thus for idealism, changes in the material world are, in the last analysis, initiated and brought about by something outside matter, not material, not subject to the laws of the material world.

But materialism traces back all change to material causes. In other words, it seeks to explain what happens in the material world from the material world itself.

But while the occurrence of change has been recognised by everyone, since none can ignore it, philosophers have nevertheless sought to find something which does not change —something permanent, something changeless, behind or within the change.

This is generally an essential part of the ideology of an exploiting class. They are afraid of change, because they are afraid that they, too, may be swept away. So they always seek for something fixed and stable, not subject to change. They try to hitch themselves on to this, as it were.

The earlier materialists, too, sought for this. Behind all the changing appearances they looked for something which never changes. But while idealists looked for the eternal and changeless in the realm of spirit, these materialists looked for it in the material world itself. And they found it in the ultimate material particle—the eternal and indestructible atom.

For such materialists, then, all *changes* were produced by the movement and interaction of *unchanging* atoms.

This is a very ancient theory, put forward over two thousand years ago in Greece, and earlier still in India.

In its day it was a very progressive theory, a great weapon against idealism and superstition. The Roman poet Lucretius, for example, explained in his philosophical poem *On the Nature of Things* that the purpose of the atomistic theory of the Greek philosopher Epicurus was to demonstrate "what are the elements out of which everything is formed, and how every-thing comes to pass without the intervention of the gods".

Thus there was born a materialism which saw the world as consisting of hard, impenetrable material particles, and which understood all change as arising from nothing but the motion and interaction of such particles.

This theory was revived in modern times. In the sixteenth and seventeenth centuries philosophers and scientists turned to it in their fight against feudal, Catholic philosophy. But this modern materialism proved to be much richer in content than the ancient. For it tried to work out what were the laws of interaction of material particles, and so to present a picture of how all phenomena, from merely physical changes to the life of man, resulted from the motion and interaction of the separate parts of matter. In this way, by the eighteenth century, there had appeared the characteristic modern theories of mechanistic materialism.

A Bourgeois Philosophy

Mechanistic materialism was in essence an ideology, a mode of theorising, of the rising bourgeoisie. In order to understand it we must understand, first of all, that it arose and developed in opposition to feudal ideology—that its critical edge was directed against feudal ideas, that it was in fact the most radical of all bourgeois forms of opposition against the feudal outlook.

In the period of the rise of the bourgeoisie, the feudal social relations were shattered, and so were the feudal ideas, embodied in the Catholic philosophy, in which those social relations were enshrined.

The feudal system, whose economic basis lay in the exploitation of the serfs by the feudal proprietors, involved complex social relationships of dependence, subordination and allegiance. All this was reflected, not only in social and political philosophy, but also in the philosophy of nature.

It was typical of the natural philosophy of the feudal period that everything in nature was explained in terms of its proper place in the system of the universe, in terms of its supposed position of dependence and subordination in that system, and of the end or purpose which it existed to serve.

The bourgeois philosophers and scientists destroyed these feudal ideas about nature. They regarded nature as a system of bodies in interaction, and, rejecting all the feudal dogmas, they called for the investigation of nature in order to discover how nature really worked.

The investigation of nature advanced hand in hand with the geographical discoveries, the development of trade and transport, the improvement of machinery and manufactures. The greatest strides were made in the mechanical sciences, closely connected as they were with the needs of technology. So it came about that materialist theory was enriched as the result of the scientific investigation of nature, and in particular by the mechanical sciences.

This determined at once the strength and the weakness, the achievement and the limitation, of the materialist theory.

What pushed that theory forward was, so Engels writes in *Ludwig Feuerbach*, "the powerful and ever more rapidly onrushing progress of science and industry". But it remained "predominantly mechanical", because only the mechanical sciences had attained any high degree of development. Its "specific, but at that time inevitable limitation" was its "exclusive application of the standards of mechanics".

The mechanistic way of understanding nature did not arise, however, simply from the fact that at that time it was only the mechanical sciences which had made any great progress. It was deeply rooted in the class outlook of the most progressive bourgeois philosophers, and this led to their turning exclusively to the mechanical sciences for their inspiration.

Just as the bourgeoisie, overthrowing feudal society, stood for individual liberty, equality and the development of a free market, so the most progressive philosophers of the bourgeoisie —the materialists—overthrowing the feudal ideas, proclaimed that the world consisted of separate material particles interacting with one another in accordance with the laws of mechanics.

This theory of nature reflected bourgeois social relations no less than the theories it replaced had reflected feudal social relations. But just as the new bourgeois social relations broke the feudal fetters and enabled a great new development of the forces of production to begin, so the corresponding bourgeois theory of nature broke down the barriers which feudal ideas had placed in the way of scientific research and enabled a great new development of scientific research to begin.

The philosophical outlook seemed to find its confirmation in science, and science provided materials for the development and working out in detail of the philosophical outlook.

The World and the Machine
The world—so thought the mechanistic materialists—consists of nothing but particles of matter in interaction. Each particle has an existence separate and distinct from every

other; in their totality they form the world; the totality of their interactions forms the totality of everything that happens in the world; and these interactions are of the mechanical type, that is to say, they consist simply of the external influence of one particle upon another.

Such a theory is equivalent to regarding the whole world as nothing but a complex piece of machinery, a mechanism.

From this standpoint, the question always posed about any part of nature is the question we ask about a machine: what is its mechanism, how does it work?

This was exemplified in Newton's account of the solar system. Newton adopted the same general view as the Greek materialist, Epicurus, in as much as he thought that the material world consisted of particles moving about in empty space. But faced with any particular natural phenomenon, such as the movements of the sun and planets, Epicurus was not in the least concerned to give any exact account of it. With regard to the apparent movement of the sun across the heavens from east to west, for example, Epicurus said that the important thing was to understand that the sun was not a god but was simply a collection of atoms: no account of the actual machinery of its motions was necessary. Perhaps, he said, the sun goes round and round the earth; but perhaps it disintegrates and its atoms separate every night, so that it is "a new sun" which we see the next morning: to him such questions were simply unimportant. Newton, on the other hand, was concerned to show exactly how the solar system worked, to demonstrate the mechanics of it, in terms of gravity and mechanical forces.

But just as Epicurus was not interested in how the solar system worked, so Newton was not interested in how it originated and developed. He took it for granted as a stable piece of machinery—created, presumably, by God. Not how it originated, not how it developed, but how it worked, was the question which he dealt with.

The same mechanistic approach was manifested in Harvey's discovery of the circulation of the blood. The essence of his discovery was that he demonstrated the mechanism of circulation, regarding the heart as a pump, which pumps the blood out along the arteries so that it flows back through the veins, the whole system being regulated by valves.

To understand the mechanistic outlook better, let us ask: what is a mechanism? what is characteristic of a mechanism?

(a) A mechanism consists of permanent parts, which fit together.

(b) It requires a motive force to set it going.

(c) Once set going, the parts interact and results are produced according to laws which can be exactly stated.

Consider, for example, such a mechanism as a watch. (a) It consists of a number of different parts—cogs, levers and so on —fitted neatly together. (b) It has to be wound up. (c) Then, as the spring uncoils, the parts interact according to laws exactly known to watchmakers, resulting in the regular movements of the hands on the dial.

Further, to know how a mechanism, such as a watch, works, you must take it to bits, find out what its parts are, how they fit together and how, by their interactions, once the mechanism is set in motion by the application of the required motive force, they produce the total motion characteristic of the mechanism in working order.

This is just how the mechanistic materialists regarded nature. They sought to take nature to bits, to find its ultimate component parts, how they fitted together and how their interactions produced all the changes we perceive, all the phenomena of the world. And moreover, finding out how the mechanism worked, they sought to find out how to repair it, how to improve it, how to change it and to make it produce new results corresponding to the requirements of man.

The Strength and Achievement of Mechanistic Materialism
Mechanistic materialism was an important milestone in our understanding of nature. And it was a great progressive step of bourgeois thinkers, a blow against idealism.

The mechanists were thorough-going in their materialism. For they waged a progressive fight against idealism and clericalism by trying to extend to the realm of mind and society the same mechanistic conceptions which were used in the scientific investigation of nature. They sought to include man and all his spiritual activities in the mechanistic system of the natural world.

The most radical mechanists regarded not merely physical processes, and not merely plant and animal life, but man himself as a machine. Already in the seventeenth century the great French philosopher Descartes had said that all animals were complicated machines—automata: but man was different, since he had a soul. But in the eighteenth century a follower of Descartes, the physician Lamettrie, wrote a book with the provocative title *Man a Machine*. Men, too, were machines, he said, though very complicated ones.

This doctrine was looked upon as exceptionally shocking, and as a terrible insult to human nature, not to mention God. Yet it was in its time a progressive view of man. The view that men are machines was an advance in the understanding of human nature as compared with the view that they are wretched pieces of clay inhabited by immortal souls. And it was, comparatively speaking, a more humane view.

For example, the great English materialist and utopian socialist Robert Owen, in his *New View of Society*, told the pious industrialists of his time:

"Experience has shown you the difference of the results between mechanism which is neat, clean, well-arranged and always in a high state of repair, and that which is allowed to be dirty, in disorder, and which therefore becomes much out of repair. . . . If, then, due care as to the state of your inanimate machines can produce such beneficial results, what may not be expected if you devote equal attention to your *vital* machines, which are far more wonderfully constructed?"

This humanitarianism was, however, at the best bourgeois humanitarianism. Like all mechanistic materialism, it was rooted in the class outlook of the bourgeoisie. The view that man is a machine is rooted in the view that in production man is a mere appendage of the machine. And if on the one hand this implies that the human machine ought to be well tended and kept in good condition, on the other hand it equally implies that no more should be expended for this purpose than is strictly necessary to keep the human machine in bare working order.

The Weakness and Limitations of Mechanistic Materialism
Mechanistic materialism had grave weaknesses.

(1) It could not sustain the materialist standpoint consistently and all the way.

For if the world is like a machine, who made it, who started it up? There was necessary, in any system of mechanistic materialism, a "Supreme Being", outside the material world —even if he no longer continuously interfered in the world and kept things moving, but did no more than start things up and then watch what happened.

Such a "Supreme Being" was postulated by nearly all the mechanistic materialists; for example, by Voltaire and Tom Paine. But this opens the door to idealism.

(2) Mechanistic materialism sees change everywhere. Yet because it always tries to *reduce* all phenomena to the same system of mechanical interactions, it sees this change as nothing but the eternal *repetition* of the same kinds of mechanical processes, an eternal cycle of the same changes.

This limitation is inseparable from the view of the world as a machine. For just as a machine has to be started up, so it can never do anything except what it was made to do. It cannot change itself or produce anything radically new. Mechanistic theory, therefore, always breaks down when it is a question of accounting for the emergence of *new quality*. It sees change everywhere—but nothing *new*, no *development*.

The various processes of nature—chemical processes and the processes of living matter, for example—cannot in fact be all reduced to one and the same kind of mechanical interaction of material particles.

Chemical interactions differ from mechanical interactions

in as much as the changes which take place as a result of chemical interaction involve a change of quality. For example, if we consider the mechanical interaction of two particles which collide, then their qualitative characteristics are irrelevant and the result is expressed as a change in the quantity and direction of motion of each. But if two chemical substances come together and combine chemically, then there results a new substance qualitatively different from either. Similarly, from the point of view of mechanics heat is nothing but an increase in the quantity of motion of the particles of matter. But in chemistry, the application of heat leads to qualitative changes.

Nor do the processes of nature consist in the repetition of the same cycle of mechanical interactions, but in nature there is continual development and evolution, producing ever new forms of the existence or, what is the same thing, motion of matter. Hence the more widely and consistently the mechanistic categories are applied in the interpretation of nature, the more is their essential limitation exposed.

(3) Still less can mechanistic materialism explain *social* development.

Mechanistic materialism expresses the radical bourgeois conception of society as consisting of social atoms, interacting together. The real economic and social causes of the development of society cannot be discovered from this point of view. And so great social changes seem to spring from quite accidental causes. Human activity itself appears to be either the mechanical result of external causes, or else it is treated—and here mechanistic materialism collapses into idealism—as purely spontaneous and uncaused.

In a word, mechanistic materialism cannot give an account of men's social activity.

Mechanistic Materialism and Utopian Socialism
The mechanistic view treated men quite abstractly, each man being regarded as a social atom endowed by nature with certain inherent properties, attributes and rights.

This was expressed in the bourgeois conception of "the

rights of man", and in the bourgeois revolutionary slogan: "All men are equal".

But the conception of human rights cannot be deduced from the abstract nature of man, but is determined by the stage of society in which men are living. Nor are men what they are "by nature", but they become what they are, and change, as a result of their social activity. Nor are all men "by nature" equal. In opposition to the bourgeois conception of abstract equality, which amounted to mere formal equality of rights as citizens, equality before the law, Marx and Engels declared that:

"the real content of the proletarian demand for equality is the demand for the abolition of classes. Any demand for equality which goes beyond that of necessity passes into absurdity" (Engels: *Anti-Dühring*, Part I, Chapter X).

Adopting their abstract, mechanistic view of men as social atoms, the progressive mechanists tried to work out, in an abstract way, what form of society would be best for mankind —what would best suit abstract human nature, as they conceived of it.

This way of thinking was taken over by the socialist thinkers who immediately preceded Marx, the utopian socialists. The utopian socialists were mechanistic materialists. They put forward socialism as an ideal society. They did not see it as necessitated by the development of the contradictions of capitalism—it could have been put forward and realised at any time, if only men had had the wit to do so. They did not see it as having to be won by working-class struggle against capitalism—it would be realised when everyone was convinced that it was just and best adapted to the requirements of human nature. (For this reason Robert Owen appealed to both the Archbishop of Canterbury and Queen Victoria to support his socialist programme.)

Again, the mechanistic materialists—and this applied above all to the utopian socialists—thought that what a man was, his character and his activities, was determined by his environment and education. Therefore they proclaimed that to make men better, happier and more rational it was simply necessary to place them in better conditions and to give them a better education.

But to this Marx replied in his *Theses on Feuerbach*:

"The materialist doctrine that men are products of circumstances and upbringing and that, therefore, changed men are produced by changed circumstances and changed upbringing, forgets that circumstances are changed precisely by men and that the educator must himself be educated."

If men are simply the products of circumstances, then they are at the mercy of circumstances. But on the contrary, men can themselves change their circumstances. And men themselves are changed, not as a mechanical result of changed circumstances, but in the course of and as a result of their own activity in changing their circumstances.

So what are the real material social causes at work in human society, which give rise to new activities, new ideas and therefore to changed circumstances and changed men?

Mechanistic materialism could not answer this question. It could not explain the laws of social development nor show how to change society.

Therefore while it was a progressive and revolutionary doctrine in its time, it could not serve to guide the struggle of the working class in striving to change society.

Chapter Four

FROM MECHANISTIC TO DIALECTICAL MATERIALISM

Things and Processes

In order to find how the limitations of the mechanist approach can be overcome we may consider first of all certain extremely dogmatic assumptions which are made by mechanistic materialism. These mechanistic assumptions are none of them justified. And by bringing them to the light of day and pointing out what is wrong with them, we can see how to advance beyond mechanistic materialism.

(1) Mechanism sees all change as having at its basis permanent and stable things with definite, fixed properties.

Thus for the mechanists the world consists of indivisible, indestructible material particles, which in their interaction manifest such properties as position, mass, velocity.

According to mechanism, if you could state the position, mass and velocity of every particle at a given instant of time, then you would have said everything that could be said about the world at that time, and could, by applying the laws of mechanics, predict everything that was going to happen afterwards.

This is the first dogmatic assumption of mechanism. But we need to reject it. For the world does not consist of *things* but of *processes*, in which things come into being and pass away.

"The world is not to be comprehended as a complex of ready-made things," wrote Engels, "but as a complex of processes, in which things apparently stable, no less than their mind-images in our heads, the concepts, go through an uninterrupted change of coming into being and passing away" (*Ludwig Feuerbach*).

This, indeed, is what science in its latest developments teaches us. Thus the atom, once thought to be eternal and indivisible, has been dissolved into electrons, protons and neutrons; and these themselves are not "fundamental particles" in any absolute sense, i.e. they are not eternal and indestructible, any more than the atom; but science more and more shows that they, too, come into being, pass away and go through many transformations.

What is fundamental is not the "thing", the "particle", but the unending *processes* of nature, in which *things* go through "an uninterrupted change of coming into being and passing away". And nature's process is, moreover, infinite: there will always be fresh aspects to be revealed, and it cannot be reduced to any *ultimate* constituents. "The electron is as inexhaustible as the atom, nature is infinite," wrote Lenin (*Materialism and Empirio-Criticism*).

Just so in considering society, we cannot understand a given society simply in terms of some set of institutions in and through which individual men and women are organised, but we must study the social processes which are going on, in the course of which both institutions and people are transformed.

Matter and Motion

(2) The second dogmatic assumption of mechanism is the assumption that no change can ever happen except by the action of some external cause.

Just as no part of a machine moves unless another part acts on it and makes it move, so mechanism sees matter as being inert—without motion, or rather without self-motion. For mechanism, nothing ever moves unless something else pushes or pulls it, it never changes unless something else interferes with it.

No wonder that, regarding matter in this way, the mechanists had to believe in a Supreme Being to give the "initial impulse".

But we need to reject this lifeless, dead theory about matter.

This theory separates matter and motion: it thinks of matter as just a dead mass, so that motion always has to be impressed on matter from outside. But, on the contrary, you cannot separate matter and motion. Motion, said Engels, is the mode of existence of matter.

"Motion is the mode of existence of matter. Never anywhere has there been matter without motion, nor can there be. Motion in cosmic space, mechanical motion of smaller masses on the various celestial bodies, the motion of molecules as heat or as electrical or magnetic currents, chemical combination or disintegration, organic life—at each given moment each individual atom of matter in the world is in one or other of these forms of motion, or in several forms of them at once. All rest, all equilibrium is only relative, and only has meaning in relation to one or other definite form of motion. A body, for example, may be on the ground in mechanical equilibrium, may be mechanically at rest; but this in no way prevents it from participating in the motion of the earth and in that of the whole solar system, just as little as it prevents its most minute parts from carrying out the oscillations determined by its temperature, or its atoms from passing through a chemical process. Matter without motion is just as unthinkable as motion without matter" (*Anti-Dühring*).

Far from being dead, lifeless, inert, it is the very nature of matter to be in process of continual change, of motion. Once we realise this, then there is an end of appeal to the "initial impulse". Motion, like matter, never had a beginning.

The conception of the inseparability of matter and motion, the understanding that "motion is the mode of existence of matter", provides the way to answering a number of perplexing questions which usually haunt people's minds when they think about materialism and which lead them to desert materialism and to run to the priests for an explanation of the "ultimate" truth about the universe.

Was the world created by a Supreme Being? What was the origin of matter? What was the origin of motion? What was the very beginning of everything? What was the first cause? These are the sort of questions which puzzle people.

It is possible to answer these questions.

No, the world was not created by a Supreme Being. Any particular organisation of matter, any particular process of matter in motion, has an origin and a beginning—it originated out of some previous organisation of matter, out of some previous process of matter in motion. But matter in motion had no origin, no beginning.

Science teaches us the inseparability of matter and motion. However static some things may seem to be, there is in them continual motion. The atom, for instance, maintains itself as the same only by means of a continual movement of its parts.

So in studying the causes of change, we should not merely seek for external causes of change, but should above all seek for the source of the change within the process itself, in its own self-movement, in the inner impulses to development contained within things themselves.

Thus in seeking the causes of social development and its laws, we should not see social changes as being brought about by the actions of great men, who impressed their superior ideas and will on the inert mass of society—nor as being brought about by accidents and external factors—but as being brought about by the development of the internal forces of society itself; and that means, by the development of the social forces of production.

Thus unlike the utopians, we see socialism as the result, not of the dreams of reformers, but of the development of capitalist society itself—which contains within itself causes which must inevitably bring it to an end and lead to the socialist revolution.

The Forms of Motion of Matter

(3) The third dogmatic assumption of mechanism is the assumption that the mechanical motion of particles, i.e. the simple change of place of particles as the result of the action on them of external forces, is the ultimate, basic form of

motion of matter; and that all changes, all happenings whatsoever can be reduced to and explained by such mechanical motion of particles.

Thus all the motion of matter is reduced to simple mechanical motion. All the changing qualities which we recognise in matter are nothing but the appearances of the basic mechanical motion of matter. However varied the appearances may be, whatever new and higher forms of development may appear to arise, they are all to be reduced to one and the same thing— the eternal repetition of the mechanical interaction of the separate parts of matter.

It is difficult to find any justification for such an assumption. In the material world there are many different types of process, which all constitute different forms of the motion of matter. But they can by no means be all reduced to one and the same form of (mechanical) motion.

"Motion in the most general sense," wrote Engels, "conceived as the mode of existence, the inherent attribute, of matter, comprehends all changes and processes occurring in the universe, from mere change of place right to thinking. The investigation of the nature of motion had as a matter of course to start from the lowest, simplest forms of this motion and to learn to grasp these before it could achieve anything in the way of explanation of the higher and more complicated forms" (*Dialectics of Nature*).

The simplest form of motion is the simple change of place of bodies, the laws of which are studied by mechanics. But that does not mean that all motion can be reduced to this simplest form of motion. It rather means that we need to study how, from the simplest form of motion, all the higher forms of motion arise and develop—"from mere change of place right to thinking".

One form of motion is transformed into another and arises from another. The higher, more complex form of motion cannot exist without the lower and simpler form: but that is not to say that it can be reduced to that simpler form. It is inseparable from the simpler form, but its nature is not exhausted thereby. For example, the thinking which goes on in our heads is inseparable from the chemical, electrical etc. motion which goes on in the grey matter of the brain; but it cannot be reduced to that motion, its nature is not exhausted thereby.

The *materialist* standpoint, however, which rejects the mechanistic idea that all forms of motion of matter can be reduced to mechanical motion, must not be confused with the *idealist* notion that the higher forms of motion cannot be explained as arising from the lower forms. For example, idealists assert that life, as a form of motion of matter, cannot possibly be derived from any processes characteristic of non-living matter. For them, life can only arise through the introduction into a material system of a mysterious something from outside—a "vital force". But to say that a higher form of motion cannot be reduced to a lower form is not to say that it cannot be derived from the lower form in the course of the latter's development. Thus materialists will always affirm that life, for example, appears at a certain stage in the development of more complex forms of non-living matter, and arises as a result of that development, not as a result of the introduction into non-living matter of a mysterious "vital force". The task of science in this sphere remains to demonstrate experimentally how the transition from non-living to living matter takes place.

Thus the mechanistic programme of reducing all the motion of matter to simple, mechanical motion must be rejected. We need rather to study all the infinitely various forms of motion of matter, in their transformations one into another, and as they arise one from another, the complex from the simple, the higher from the lower.

In the case of society, no one has yet tried to show how social changes can be explained by the mechanical interactions of the atoms composing the bodies of the various members of society—though to do so would be the logical culmination of the mechanistic programme. But the next best thing is attempted by the mechanistic theory known as "economic

45

determinism". According to this theory, the whole motion of society is to be explained by the economic changes taking place in society, all the determinants of social change have been exhausted when the economic process has been described. This is an example of the mechanistic programme of reducing a complex motion to a single simple form—the process of social change, including all the political, cultural and ideological developments, to a simple economic process. But the task of explaining social development cannot be fulfilled by trying to reduce the whole development to an economic process. The task is rather to show how, on the basis of the economic process, all the various forms of social activity arise and play their part in the complex movement of society.

Things and their Interconnection

(4) The last dogmatic assumption of mechanism to be mentioned is that each of the things or particles, whose interactions are said to make up the totality of events in the universe, has its own fixed nature quite independent of everything else. In other words, each thing can be considered as existing in separation from other things, as an independent unit.

Proceeding on this assumption it follows that all relations between things are merely external relations. That is to say, things enter into various relationships one with another, but these relationships are accidental and make no difference to the nature of the things related.

And regarding each thing as a separate unit entering into external relations with other things, it further follows that mechanism regards the whole as no more than the sum of its separate parts. According to this view, the properties and laws of development of the whole are uniquely determined by the properties of all its parts.

Not one of these assumptions is correct. Nothing exists or can exist in splendid isolation, separate from its conditions of existence, independent of its relationships with other things. Things come into being, exist and cease to exist, not each independent of all other things, but each in its relationship with other things. The very nature of a thing is modified and transformed by its relationships with other things. When things enter into such relationships that they become parts of a whole, the whole cannot be regarded as nothing more than the sum total of the parts. True, the whole is nothing apart from and independent of its parts. But the mutual relations which the parts enter into in constituting the whole modify their own properties, so that while it may be said that the whole is determined by the parts it may equally be said that the parts are determined by the whole.

Once again, the development of science itself shows the inadmissibility of the old mechanistic assumptions. These assumptions have force only in the very limited sphere of the study of the mechanical interactions of discrete particles. In physics they were already shattered with the development of the study of the electro-magnetic field. Still less are they admissible in biology, in the study of living matter. And still less are they admissible in the study of men and society. We cannot understand social processes, as mechanists always try to do, as resulting simply from a set of fixed characteristics of "human nature". For "human nature" is always conditioned by and in various respects changes with changes in men's social relations.

The Correction of Mechanistic Materialism
When we bring into the open and reject these assumptions of mechanistic materialism, then we begin to see the need for a materialist doctrine of a different, of a new type—a materialism which overcomes the weaknesses and narrow, dogmatic assumptions of mechanism.

This is dialectical materialism.

Dialectical materialism understands the world, not as a complex of ready-made things, but as a complex of processes, in which all things go through an uninterrupted change of coming into being and passing away.

Dialectical materialism considers that matter is always in motion, that motion is the mode of existence of matter, so that there can no more be matter without motion than motion without matter. Motion does not have to be impressed upon matter by some outside force, but above all it is necessary to look for the inner impulses of development, the self-motion, inherent in all processes.

Dialectical materialism understands the motion of matter as comprehending all changes and processes in the universe, from mere change of place right to thinking. It recognises, therefore, the infinite diversity of the forms of motion of matter, the transformation of one form into another, the development of the forms of motion of matter from the simple to the complex, from the lower to the higher.

Dialectical materialism considers that, in the manifold processes taking place in the universe, things come into being, change and pass out of being, not as separate individual units, but in essential relation and interconnection, so that they cannot be understood each separately and by itself but only in their relation and interconnection.

In dialectical materialism, therefore, there is established a materialist conception far richer in content and more comprehensive than the former mechanistic materialism.

Chapter Five

THE DIALECTICAL CONCEPTION OF DEVELOPMENT

The Idea of Evolution

We have seen that the corrections of the mechanistic standpoint made by dialectical materialism are fully justified by and have a basis in the advance of science. Indeed, the advance of science itself has shattered the whole conception of the universe held by the older, mechanistic materialists.

According to that conception, the universe always remained much the same. It was a huge machine which always did the same things, kept grinding out the same products, went on and on in a perpetual cycle of the same processes.

Thus it used to be thought that the stars and the solar system always remained the same—and that the earth, with its continents and oceans and the plants and animals inhabiting them, likewise always remained the same.

But this conception has given way to the conception of evolution, which has invaded all spheres of investigation without exception. Science, however, does not advance in isolation from society as a whole, and the widespread application of the idea of evolution was due not simply to its verification in scientific theory but also to its popularity with the new, rising forces of industrial capitalism, themselves the patrons of science.

"The bourgeoisie cannot exist without constantly revolutionising the instruments of production, and thereby the relations of production, and with them the whole relations of society. Conservation of the old modes of production in unaltered form was, on the contrary, the first condition of existence of all earlier industrial classes. Constant revolutionising of production, uninterrupted disturbance of all social conditions, everlasting uncertainty and agitation, distinguish the bourgeois epoch from all earlier ones" (Marx and Engels: *Manifesto of the Communist Party*).

The industrial capitalists saw themselves as the bearers of progress. And as they thought progress was the law of capitalism, so they saw it as the law of the whole universe.

So there was made possible a great advance in the scientific picture of the universe. We find developing a picture of the universe, not as static, as always the same, but as in continual progressive development.

The stars did not always exist—they were formed out of masses of dispersed gas.

Once formed, the whole stellar system, with all the stars in it, goes through an evolutionary process, stage by stage.

Some stars, like our sun, acquire planets—a solar system. Thus the earth was born. As its surface cooled, so chemical compounds were formed, impossible in the high temperatures of the stars.

Thus matter began to manifest new properties, non-existent before—the properties of chemical combination.

Then organic compounds were formed out of the complex linking of carbon atoms. And from organic matter the first bodies arose which began to manifest the properties of life, of living matter. Still new properties of matter emerged—the properties of living matter.

Living organisms went through a long evolution, leading eventually to man. With man, human society was born. And still new processes, with new laws, arose—the laws of society, and the laws of thought.

What comes next?

Capitalist science can go no further. Here it ends, since capitalist science cannot contemplate the ending of capitalism. But socialist science shows that man himself is about to embark on a new phase of evolution—communist society, in which the whole social process will be brought under his own conscious, planned direction.

All this is the evolutionary history of the material universe.

Apart from the last point, it may be said this is all common knowledge. Bourgeois thinkers know this as well as Marxists, though they often forget it. But Marxism does not only stress the fact that everything in the world goes through a process of development. What Marxism found out was how to understand and explain this development in a materialist way.

Marx's scientific discoveries about the laws of development of society were made by applying the conceptions of materialist dialectics. That is why Marxism alone is able to give a fully scientific account of development and to point out the future path.

Marx demonstrated how to understand all change and development, in nature and in society, in a materialist way, and therefore how to become masters of the future.

Idealist Conceptions of Change and Development
How did bourgeois thinkers try to account for the universal change and development which they discovered?

Let us consider what some of them have had to say over a period of more than a century.

Hegel said that the whole process of development taking place in history was due to the Absolute Idea realising itself in history. Herbert Spencer said that all development was a process of increasing "integration of matter", and he put this down to what he called an "Incomprehensible and Omnipresent Power". Henri Bergson said that everything was in process of evolution, due to the activity of "the Life Force". Fairly recently, a school of British philosophers has coined the phrase "emergent evolution". They pointed out that in the course of development new qualities of matter are continually emerging, one after the other. But as to why this should happen, one of the leaders of this school, Professor Samuel Alexander, said that it was inexplicable and must be accepted "with natural piety", while another of its leaders, Professor C. Lloyd Morgan, said that it must be due to some immanent force at work in the world, which he identified with God.

51

Thus in every case some fantasy, something inexplicable and unpredictable, was conjured up to explain development. And so, when they thought about the future, all these bourgeois philosophers of evolution either thought, like Hegel, that development had now finished (Hegel taught that the Absolute Idea was fully realised in the Prussian State of which he was a distinguished employee), or else regarded the future as unfathomable.

Nowadays they begin to give up hope altogether and regard everything—past, present and future—as incomprehensible, the result of forces no one can ever understand or control.

A second defect in the evolutionary ideas of most bourgeois thinkers is that they regard the process of evolution as a smooth, continuous and unbroken process. They see the process of transition from one evolutionary stage to another as taking place through a series of gradations, without conflict and without any break in continuity.

But continuity is not the law of development. On the contrary, periods of smooth, continuous evolutionary development are interrupted by sudden and abrupt changes. The emergence of the new stage in development takes place, when the conditions for it have matured, by a break in continuity, by the leap from one state to another.

Hegel was the first to point this out.

With every period of transition, he observed:

"it is as in the case of the birth of a child; after a long period of nutrition in silence, the continuity of the gradual growth in size, of quantitative change, is suddenly cut short by the first breath drawn—there is a break in the process, a qualitative change—and the child is born" (*Phenomenology of Mind*).

But Marx alone followed up this profound observation of Hegel. As for the ensuing bourgeois thinkers, although the investigations of science, and common experience itself, clearly demonstrate that development cannot take place without discontinuity, without abrupt transitions and the leap from one state to another, they have nevertheless in their general theories tried to make unbroken continuity the law of evolution.

This prejudice in favour of a smooth line of evolution has gone hand in hand with the liberal belief that capitalist society will evolve smoothly—through orderly bourgeois progress broadening down "from precedent to precedent", as Tennyson once expressed it. To have thought differently about evolution in general would have implied that we would have to think differently about social evolution in particular.

The Dialectical Materialist Conception of Development
The problem of understanding and explaining development in a materialist way—that is, "in harmony with the facts conceived in their own and not in a fantastic connection"—is answered by dialectical materialism.

Dialectical materialism considers the universe, not as static, not as unchanging, but as in continual process of development. It considers this development, not as a smooth, continuous and unbroken process, but as a process in which phases of gradual evolutionary change are interrupted by breaks in continuity, by the sudden leap from one state to another. And it seeks for the explanation, the driving force, of this universal movement, not in inventions of idealist fantasy, but within material processes themselves—in the inner contradictions, the opposite conflicting tendencies, which are in operation in every process of nature and society.

The main ideas of materialist dialectics, which are applied in dealing with the laws of development of the real material world, including society, will be the subject of the following chapters. But this is how Lenin summed them up in his *Philosophical Notebooks*.

The essential idea of materialist dialectics is:

"the recognition of the contradictory, mutually exclusive, opposite tendencies in all phenomena and processes of nature. . . . This alone furnishes the key to the self-movement of everything in existence. It alone furnishes the key

53

to the leaps, to the break in continuity, to the transformation into the opposite, to the destruction of the old and emergence of the new. . . .

In its proper meaning, dialectics is the study of the contradiction within the very essence of things.

Development is the struggle of opposites."

Where contradiction is at work, there is the force of development.

This materialist understanding of dialectics is the key to understanding the forces of development within the material world itself, without recourse to outside causes.

This discovery arises from the whole advance of science and philosophy.

But above all it arises from the investigation of the laws of society, an investigation made imperative thanks to the very development of society—from the discovery of the contradictions of capitalism, explaining the forces of social development, and thereby showing the way forward from capitalism to socialism.

That is why bourgeois thinkers could not answer the problem of explaining the real material forces of development in nature and society. To answer this problem was to condemn the capitalist system. And here they had a blind spot. Only the revolutionary philosophy of the vanguard of the revolutionary class, the working class, could do it.

Marx's discovery of the laws of materialist dialectics showed us how to understand the dialectical development of nature. But above all it showed us how to understand social change and how to wage the working-class struggle for socialism.

This discovery revolutionised philosophy.

It signalised the triumph of materialism over idealism, by doing away with the limitations of the merely mechanistic materialism of the past.

It likewise spelled the end of all "systems" of philosophy.

It made philosophy into a revolutionary weapon of the working people, an instrument, a method for understanding the world so as to change it.

PART TWO

DIALECTICS

Chapter Six

DIALECTICS AND METAPHYSICS

The Metaphysical Way of Thinking
We have seen how materialist explanation is opposed to idealist explanation. And then we saw how materialists formerly interpreted things in a mechanist way, but how mechanistic materialism proved inadequate to explain real processes of change and development. For this we need materialist dialectics. We need to study and understand things dialectically.

The dialectical method is, indeed, nothing but the method of studying and understanding things in their real change and development.

As such, it stands opposed to *metaphysics*.

What is metaphysics? Or more exactly, what is the metaphysical way of thinking, which is opposed by the dialectical way of thinking?

Metaphysics is essentially an abstract way of thinking. In a sense all thinking is "abstract", since it works with general concepts and cannot but disregard a great deal of particular and unessential detail. For example, if we say that "men have two legs", we are thinking of the two-leggedness of men in abstraction from their other properties, such as having a head, two arms and so on; and similarly we are thinking of all men in general, disregarding the individuality of particular men. But there is abstraction and abstraction. Metaphysical abstraction consists of thinking as though what is abstracted could exist in abstraction. The art of right thinking involves learning how to avoid metaphysical abstraction.

Suppose, for example, we are thinking about men, about

"human nature". Then we should think about human nature in such a way that we recognise that men live in society and that their human nature cannot be independent of their living in society but develops and changes with the development of society. We shall then form ideas about human nature which correspond to the actual conditions of men's existence and to their change and development. But yet people often think about "human nature" in a very different way, as though there were such a thing as "human nature" which manifested itself quite independent of the actual conditions of human existence and which was always and everywhere exactly the same. To think in such a way is obviously to think in a misleadingly abstract way. And it is just such a misleadingly abstract way of thinking that we call "metaphysics".

The concept of fixed, unchanging "human nature" is an example of metaphysical abstraction, of the metaphysical way of thinking.

The metaphysician does not think in terms of real *men*, but of "Man" in the abstract.

Metaphysics, or the metaphysical way of thinking, is, then, that way of thinking which thinks of things (1) in abstraction from their conditions of existence, and (2) in abstraction from their change and development. It thinks of things (1) in separation one from another, ignoring their interconnections, and (2) as fixed and frozen, ignoring their change and development.

One example of metaphysics has already been given. It is not difficult to find plenty more. Indeed, the metaphysical way of thinking is so widespread, and has become so much part and parcel of current bourgeois ideology, that there is hardly an article in a journal, a television discussion, or a book by a learned professor, in which examples of metaphysical fallacy are not to be found.

A good deal is said and written, for example, about democracy. But the speakers and writers usually refer to some pure or absolute democracy, which they seek to define in abstraction from the actual development of society, of classes and of class struggle. But there can be no such pure democracy; it is a metaphysical abstraction. If we want to understand democracy we have always to ask: democracy for whom, for the exploiters or the exploited? We have to understand that since democracy is a form of government, there is no democracy which is not associated with the rule of some particular class, and that the democracy which is established when the working class is the ruling class is a higher form of democracy than capitalist democracy, just as capitalist democracy is a higher form of democracy than, say, the slave-owners' democracy of ancient Greece. In other words, we should not try to think of democracy in abstraction from real social relations and from the real change and development of society.

Again, up to recently most British children were regularly subjected to "intelligence tests". It was alleged that each child possessed a certain fixed quantity of "intelligence", which could be estimated without regard to the actual conditions of the child's existence and which determined his capabilities throughout the whole of his life regardless of whatever conditions for change and development might subsequently come his way. This is another example of metaphysics. In this case the metaphysical conception of "intelligence" was used as an excuse for denying educational opportunities to the majority of children on the grounds that their intelligence was too low for them to benefit from such opportunities.

In general, metaphysics is a way of thinking which tries to fix the nature, properties and potentialities of everything it considers once and for all: it presupposes that each thing has a fixed nature and fixed properties.

And it thinks in terms of "things" rather than "processes". It tries to sum up everything in a formula, which says that the whole world, or any part of the world which is under consideration, consists of just such and such things with such and such properties. Such a formula we may call a "metaphysical" formula.

In philosophy, metaphysics often means the search for the "ultimate constituents of the universe". Thus the materialists who said that the ultimate constituents were small, solid, material particles were just as much metaphysicians as the idealists who said that the ultimate constituents were spirits. All such philosophers thought they could sum up "the ultimate nature of the universe" in some formula. Some have had this formula, some that, but all have been metaphysicians. Yet it has been a hopeless quest. We cannot sum up the whole infinite changing universe in any such formula. And the more we find out about it, the more is this evident.

It should now be clear that the mechanistic materialism which we discussed in the preceding chapters can equally well be called *metaphysical* materialism.

We may also note, in passing, that certain philosophers today, the so-called positivists, who say we have no right to assert that anything exists except our own sense-perceptions, claim to be against "metaphysics" because they claim to reject any philosophy which seeks for "the ultimate constituents of the universe". For them, "metaphysics" means any theory which deals with "ultimates" not verifiable in sense-experience. By using the term in this way, they conceal the fact that they themselves are, if anything, more metaphysical than any other philosophers. For their own mode of thinking reaches extremes of metaphysical abstraction. What could be more metaphysical than to imagine, as the positivist philosophers do, that our sense-experience exists in abstraction from the real material world outside us? Indeed, they themselves make "sense-experience" into a metaphysical "ultimate".

In opposition to the abstract, metaphysical way of thinking, dialectics teaches us to think of things in their real changes and interconnections. To think dialectically is to think concretely, and to think concretely is to think dialectically. When we oppose the dialectical method to metaphysics, then we show up the inadequacy, one-sidedness or falsity of the abstractions of metaphysics.

This consideration enables us to understand the original meaning of the term "dialectics". The word is derived from the Greek *dialego*, meaning to discuss or debate. It was considered that to discuss a question from all sides, and from all angles, allowing different one-sided points of view to oppose and contradict each other during the debate, was the best method of arriving at the truth. Such was the dialectics employed, for example, by Socrates. When anyone claimed to have a formula which answered some question once and for all, Socrates would enter into discussion with him and, by forcing him to consider the question from different angles, would compel him to contradict himself and so to admit that his formula was false. By this method Socrates considered that it was possible to arrive at more adequate ideas about things.

The Marxist dialectical method develops from and includes dialectics in the sense in which it was understood by the Greeks. But it is far richer in content, far wider in its scope. As a result, it becomes something qualitatively *new* as compared with pre-Marxist dialectics—a new revolutionary method. For it is combined with a consistent materialism, and ceases to be a mere method of argument, becoming a method of investigation applicable to both nature and society, a method of materialist understanding of the world which grows out of and guides the activity of changing the world.

The Metaphysical "Either-Or"

Metaphysics presupposes that each thing has its own fixed nature, its own fixed properties, and considers each thing by itself, in isolation. It tries to settle the nature and properties of each thing as a given, separate object of investigation, not considering things in their interconnection and in their change and development.

Because of this, metaphysics thinks of things in terms of hard and fast antitheses. It opposes things of one sort to things of another sort: if a thing is of one sort, it has one set of properties; if of another sort, it has another set of properties; the one excludes the other, and each is thought of in separation from the other.

Thus Engels writes in his introduction to *Anti-Dühring*:

"To the metaphysician, things and their mental images, ideas, are isolated, to be considered one after the other, apart from each other, rigid fixed objects of investigation given once and for all. He thinks in absolutely irreconcilable

61

antitheses. 'His communication is Yea, yea, Nay, nay, for whatever is more than these cometh of evil.' For him a thing either exists or it does not exist; it is equally impossible for a thing to be itself and at the same time something else."

Philosophers have expressed the essence of this metaphysical way of thinking in the formula: "Each thing is what it is, and not another thing." This may sound no more than plain common sense. But that only shows that so-called common sense itself conceals misleading ideas which need to be brought into the open. This way of thinking prevents us from studying things in their real changes and interconnections—in all their contradictory aspects and relationships, in their process of changing from "one thing" into "another thing".

It is not only philosophers who are metaphysicians.

There are left-wing trade unionists, for example, who are as metaphysical as any school of philosophers. For them everyone at their trade union branch meeting is either a class-conscious militant or else he is a right-wing opportunist. Everyone must fit into one or other category, and once he is down as "right wing" he is finished so far as they are concerned. That some worker who has been their opponent in the past and on some issues may yet prove an ally in the future and on other issues is not allowed for in their metaphysical outlook on life.

In one of Molière's plays there is a man who learns for the first time about prose. When they explain to him what prose is, he exclaims: "Why, I've been speaking prose all my life!"

Similarly, there are many workers who may well say: "Why, I've been a metaphysician all my life!"

The metaphysician has his formula ready for everything. He says—either this formula fits or it does not. If it does, that settles it. If it does not, then he has some alternative formula ready. "Either-or, but not both" is his motto. A thing is either this or that; it has either this set of properties or that set of properties; two things stand to one another either in this relationship or in that.

The use of the metaphysical "either-or" leads people into countless difficulties.

For example, difficulties are felt in understanding the relations between American and British imperialism today. For it is argued: either they are working together, or else they are not. If they are working together, then there is no rift between them; if there is a rift between them, then they are not working together. But on the contrary, they are working together and yet there are rifts between them; and we cannot understand the way they work together nor fight them effectively unless we understand the rifts which divide them.

Again, difficulties are felt in understanding the possibility of the peaceful co-existence of capitalist and socialist states. For it is argued: either they can co-exist peacefully, in which case antagonism between capitalism and socialism must cease; or else the antagonism remains, in which case they cannot co-exist peacefully. But on the contrary, the antagonism remains, and yet the striving of the socialist states and of millions of people in all countries for peace can lead to peaceful relations between capitalist and socialist states.

It is often difficult to avoid a metaphysical way of thinking. And this is because, misleading as it is, it yet has its roots in something very necessary and useful.

It is necessary for us to classify things—to have some system of classifying them and assigning their properties and relations. That is a prerequisite of clear thinking. We have to work out what different kinds of things there are in the world, to say that these have these properties as distinct from those which have those other properties, and to say what are their relations.

But when we go on to consider these things and properties and relations each in isolation, as fixed constants, as mutually exclusive terms, then we begin to go wrong. For everything in the world has many different and indeed contradictory aspects, exists in intimate relationship with other things and not in isolation, and is subject to change. And so it frequently happens that when we classify something as "A" and not "B" then this formula is upset by its changing from "A" to "B", or by its being "A" in some relationships and "B" in others, or by its having a contradictory nature, part "A" and part "B".

For example, we all know the difference between birds and mammals, and that while birds lay eggs mammals, in general, produce their young alive and suckle them. Naturalists used to believe that mammals were rigidly distinguished from birds because, amongst other things, mammals do not lay eggs. But this formula was completely upset when an animal called the platypus was discovered, for while the platypus is undoubtedly a mammal, it is a mammal which lays eggs. What is the explanation of this irregular behaviour of the platypus? It is to be found in the evolutionary relationship of birds and mammals, which are both descended from original egg-laying animals. The birds have continued to lay eggs while the mammals stopped doing so—except for a few conservative animals like the platypus. If we think of animals in their evolution, their development, this appears very natural. But if we try, as the older naturalists tried, to make them fit into some rigid, fixed scheme of classification, then the products of evolution upset that classification.

Again, an idea or a theory which was progressive in one set of circumstances, when it first arose, cannot for that reason be labelled "progressive" in an absolute sense, since it may later become reactionary in new circumstances. For instance, mechanisitc materialism when it first arose was a progressive theory. But we cannot say that it is still progressive today. On the contrary, under the new circumstances which have arisen mechanistic theory has become retrograde, reactionary. Mechanism, which was progressive in the rising phase of capitalism, goes hand in hand with idealism as part of the ideology of capitalism in decay.

Common sense, too, recognises the limitations of the metaphysical way of thinking.

For example: When is a man bald? Common sense recognises that though we can distinguish bald men from non-bald men, nevertheless baldness develops through a process of losing one's hair, and therefore men in the midst of this process enter into a phase in which we cannot say absolutely either that they are bald or that they are not: they are in process of becoming bald. The metaphysical "either-or" breaks down.

In all these examples we are confronted with the distinction between an *objective process*, in which something undergoes change, and the *concepts* in terms of which we try to sum up the characteristics of the things involved in the process. Such concepts never do and never can always and in all respects correspond to their objects, precisely because the objects are undergoing change.

Engels explained this in a letter (March 12, 1895) to a certain Mr. C. Schmidt, who was puzzled by it:

"Are the concepts that prevail in natural science fictions because they by no means always coincide with reality? From the moment we accept the theory of evolution all our concepts of organic life correspond only approximately to reality. Otherwise there would be no change; on the day that concept and reality absolutely coincide in the organic world, development is at an end."

And he pointed out that similar considerations apply to all concepts without exception.

The Unity and Struggle of Opposites

When we think of the properties of things, their relationships, their modes of action and interaction, the processes into which they enter, then we find that, generally speaking, all these properties, relationships, interactions and processes divide into *fundamental opposites*.

For example, if we think of the simplest ways in which two bodies can act on one another, then we find that this action is either repulsion or attraction.

If we consider the electical properties of bodies, then there is positive and negative electricity.

In organic life, there is the building up of organic compounds and the breaking of them down.

Again, in mathematics, there is addition and subtraction, plus and minus.

65

And in general, whatever sphere of inquiry we may be considering, we find that it involves such fundamental opposites. We find ourselves considering, not just a number of *different* things, *different* properties, *different* relations, *different* processes, but pairs of *opposites*, fundamental *oppositions*. As Hegel put it: "In opposition, the different is not confronted by any other, but by *its* other" (*Encyclopaedia of Philosophical Sciences: Logic*, Section 119).

Thus if we think of the forces acting between two bodies, there are not just a number of different forces, but they divide into attractive and repulsive forces; if we think of electric charges, there are not just a number of different charges, but they divide into positive and negative; and so on. Attraction stands opposed to repulsion, positive electricity to negative electricity.

Such fundamental oppositions are not understood by the metaphysical way of thinking.

In the first place, the metaphysical way of thinking tries to ignore and discount opposition. It seeks to understand a given subject-matter simply in terms of a whole number of different properties and different relations of things, ignoring the fundamental oppositions which are manifested in these properties and relations. Thus those who think in metaphysical terms about class-divided societies, for example, try to understand society as consisting merely of a large number of different individuals connected together by all kinds of different social relations—but they ignore the fundamental opposition of exploiters and exploited, manifested in all those social relations.

In the second place, when the metaphysical way of thinking does nevertheless come upon the fundamental oppositions and cannot ignore them, then—true to its habit of thinking of each thing in isolation, as a fixed constant—it considers these opposites each in isolation from the other, understands them separately and as each excluding the other. Thus, for example, the older physicists used to think of positive and negative electricity just simply as two different "electrical fluids".

But contrary to metaphysics, not only are fundamental

opposites involved in every subject-matter, but these opposites mutually imply each other, are inseparably connected together, and, far from being exclusive, neither can exist or be understood except in relation to the other.

This characteristic of opposition is known as polarity: fundamental opposites are polar opposites. A magnet, for example, has two poles, a north pole and a south pole. But these poles, opposite and distinct, cannot exist in separation. If the magnet is cut in two, there is not a north pole in one half and a south pole in the other, but north and south poles recur in each half. The north pole exists only as the opposite of the south, and vice versa; the one can be defined only as the opposite of the other.

In general, fundamental opposition has to be understood as polar opposition, and every subject-matter has to be understood in terms of the polar opposition involved in it.

Thus in physics we find that attraction and repulsion are involved in every physical process in such a way that they cannot be separated or isolated the one from the other. In considering living bodies, we do not find in some cases the building up of organic compounds and in other cases their breaking down, but every life process involves both the building up and the breaking down of organic compounds. In capitalist society the increasing socialisation of labour is inseparable from its opposite, the increasing centralisation of capital.

This unity of opposites—the fact that opposites cannot be understood in separation one from another, but only in their inseparable connection in every field of investigation—is strikingly exemplified in mathematics. Here the fundamental operations are the two oppositions, addition and subtraction. And so far is it from being the case that addition and subtraction can be understood each apart from the other, that addition can be represented as subtraction and vice versa; thus the operation of subtraction $(a-b)$ can be represented as an addition $(-b+a)$. Similarly a division a/b can be represented as a multiplication $a \times (1/b)$ (Engels: *Dialectics of Nature*, "Note on Mathematics").

The unity of opposites, their inseparable connection, is by

no means to be understood as a harmonious and stable relationship, as a state of equilibrium. On the contrary. "The unity of opposites is conditional, temporary, transitory, relative. The struggle of mutually exclusive opposites is absolute, just as development and motion are absolute" (Lenin: *Philosophical Notebooks*).

The existence of fundamental polar oppositions, manifesting themselves in every department of nature and society, expresses itself in the *conflict* and *struggle* of opposed tendencies, which, despite phases of temporary equilibrium, lead to continual motion and development, to a perpetual coming into being and passing away of everything in existence, to sharp changes of state and transformations.

Thus, for example, the equilibrium of attractive and repulsive forces in the physical world is never more than conditional and temporary; the conflict and struggle of attraction and repulsion always asserts itself, issuing in physical changes and transformations, whether transformations on an atomic scale, chemical changes or, on a grand scale, in the explosion of stars.

Dialectics and Metaphysics
To sum up.

Metaphysics thinks in terms of "ready-made" things, whose properties and potentialities it seeks to fix and determine once and for all. It considers each thing by itself, in isolation from every other, in terms of irreconcilable antitheses—"either-or". It contrasts one thing to another, one property to another, one relationship to another, not considering things in their real movement and interconnection, and not considering that every subject-matter represents a unity of opposites—opposed but inseparably connected together.

Contrary to metaphysics, dialectics refuses to think of things each by itself, as having a fixed nature and fixed properties—"either-or"—but it recognises that things come into being, exist and cease to be in a process of unending change and development, in a process of complicated and ever-changing inter-relationship, in which each thing exists only in

68

its connection with other things and goes through a series of transformations, and in which is always manifested the unity, inseparable interconnection and struggle of the opposite properties, aspects, tendencies characteristic of every phenomenon of nature and society.

Contrary to metaphysics, the aim of dialectics is to trace the real changes and interconnections in the world and to think of things always in their motion and interconnection.

Thus Engels writes in *Ludwig Feuerbach*:

"The world is not to be comprehended as a complex of ready-made things but as a complex of processes. . . . One no longer permits oneself to be imposed upon by the antitheses insuperable for the old metaphysics. . . ."

And in *Anti-Dühring*:

"The old rigid antitheses, the sharp impassible dividing lines are more and more disappearing. . . . The recognition that these antitheses and distinctions are in fact to be found in nature but only with relative validity, and that on the other hand their imagined rigidity and absoluteness have been introduced into nature only by our minds—this recognition is the kernel of the dialectical conception of nature.

Dialectics . . . grasps things and their images, ideas, essentially in their inter-connection, in their sequence, their movement, their birth and death. . . ."

Lenin wrote in his *Philosophical Notebooks* that the understanding of the "contradictory parts" of every phenomenon was "the essence of dialectics". It consists in "the recognition (discovery) of the contradictory, mutually exclusive, opposite tendencies in all phenomena and processes of nature, including mind and society".

Lastly, Marx in the Preface to *Capital* wrote that:

"dialectic . . . in its rational form is a scandal and abomination to bourgeoisdom and its doctrinaire professors, because

69

it includes in its comprehension and affirmative recognition of the existing state of things, at the same time also, the recognition of the negation of that state, of its inevitable breaking up; because it regards every historically developed social form as in fluid movement, and therefore takes into account its transient nature not less than its momentary existence; because it lets nothing impose upon it, and is in its essence critical and revolutionary."

Chapter Seven

CHANGE AND INTERCONNECTION

The Dialectical versus the Metaphysical Way of Thinking
In a widely circulated booklet on *Dialectical and Historical Materialism* Stalin included a useful account of four of the ways in which a dialectical approach differs from a metaphysical one.

(1) Contrary to metaphysics, dialectics does not regard nature as just an agglomeration of things, each existing independently of the others, but it considers things as "connected with, dependent on and determined by each other". Hence it considers that nothing can be understood taken by itself, in isolation, but must always be understood "in its inseparable connection with other things, and as conditioned by them".

(2) Contrary to metaphysics, dialectics considers everything as in "a state of continuous movement and change, of renewal and development, where something is always arising and developing and something always disintegrating and dying away". Hence it considers things "not only from the standpoint of their interconnection and interdependence, but also from the standpoint of their movement, their change, their development, their coming into being and going out of being".

(3) Contrary to metaphysics, dialectics does not regard the process of development as "a simple process of growth", but as "a development which passes from . . . quantitative changes to open, fundamental changes, to qualitative changes", which occur "abruptly, taking the form of a leap from one state to another". Hence it considers development as "an onward and upward movement, as a transition from an old qualitative state to a new qualitative state, as a development from the simple to the complex, from the lower to the higher".

(4) Contrary to metaphysics, dialectics "holds that the process of development from the lower to the higher takes place . . . as a disclosure of the contradictions inherent in things . . . as a struggle of opposite tendencies which operate on the basis of these contradictions".

We shall postpone until the next chapter consideration of the process of development from one qualitative state to another. In this chapter we shall look at the significance of always considering things in their interconnection and in their movement and change.

Considering Things in Their Interconnection and Circumstances
The dialectical method demands, first, that we should consider things, not each by itself, but always in their interconnection with other things.

This sounds "obvious". Nevertheless it is an "obvious" principle which is very often ignored and is extremely important to remember. We have already considered it and some examples of its application in discussing metaphysics, since the very essence of metaphysics is to think of things in an abstract way, isolated from their relations with other things and from the concrete circumstances in which they exist.

The principle of considering things in relation to actual conditions and circumstances, and not apart from those actual conditions and circumstances, is always of fundamental importance for the working-class movement in deciding the most elementary questions of policy.

For example, there was a time when the British workers were fighting for a ten-hour day. They were right at that time not to make their immediate demand an eight-hour day, since this was not yet a realisable demand. They were equally right, when they got a ten-hour day, not to be satisfied with it.

There are times when it is correct for a section of workers to come out on strike, and there are times when it is not correct. Such matters have to be judged according to the actual circumstances of the case. Similarly there are times when it is correct to go on prolonging and extending a strike, and there are times when it is correct to call it off.

No working-class leader can be of very much use if he tries to decide questions of policy in terms of "general principle" alone, without taking into account the actual circumstances in relation to which policy has to be operated, without understanding that the same policy can be right in one case and wrong in another, depending on the concrete circumstances of each case.

Thus in *Left-Wing Communism* Lenin wrote:

> "Of course, in politics, in which sometimes extremely complicated—national and international—relationships between classes and parties have to be dealt with . . . it would be absurd to concoct a recipe, or general rule . . . that would serve in all cases. One must have the brains to analyse the situation in each separate case."

This readiness on the part of Marxists to adapt policy to circumstances and to change policy with circumstances is sometimes called Communist "opportunism". But it is nothing of the kind—or rather, it is the very opposite. It is the application in practice of the science of the strategy and tactics of working-class struggle. Indeed, what is meant by opportunism in relation to working-class policy? It means subordinating the long-term interests of the working class as a whole to the temporary interests of a section, sacrificing the interests of the class to defence of the temporary privileges of some particular group. Communists are guided by the principle stated in *The Communist Manifesto*, that "they always and everywhere represent the interests of the movement as a whole". And this requires that, in the interests of the movement as a whole, one must analyse the situation in each separate case, deciding what policy to pursue in each case in the light of the concrete circumstances.

On general questions, too, the greatest confusion can arise from forgetting the dialectical principle that things must not be considered in isolation but in their inseparable interconnection.

For example, the British Labour leaders once said, and many members of the Labour Party continue to say, that nationalisation is an instalment of socialism. They consider nationalisation by itself, in isolation, out of connection with the state and with the social structure in relation to which nationalisation measures are introduced. They overlook the fact that if the public power, the state, remains in the hands of the exploiters, and if their representatives sit on and control the boards of the nationalised industries, which continue to be run on the basis of exploiting the labour of one class for the profit of another class, then nationalisation is not socialism. Socialist nationalisation can come into being only when the public power, the state, is in the hands of the workers.

Again, in political arguments people very often appeal to a concept of "fairness" which leads them to judge events without the slightest consideration of the real meaning of those events, of the circumstances in which they occur. What's sauce for the goose is sauce for the gander: that is the principle employed in such arguments.

Thus it is argued that if we defend the democratic right of the workers in a capitalist country to agitate for the ending of capitalism and the introduction of socialism, then we cannot deny to others in a socialist country the right to agitate for the ending of socialism and the reintroduction of capitalism. Those who argue like this throw up their hands in horror when they find that former groupings in the U.S.S.R., who sought to restore capitalism in that country, were deprived of the possibility of carrying out their aims, and that later the same thing happened to groupings with similar aims in Hungary. Why, they exclaim, this is undemocratic, this is tyranny! Such an argument overlooks the difference between fighting in the interests of the vast majority of the people to end exploitation, and fighting in the interests of a small section to preserve or reintroduce exploitation; it overlooks the difference between defending the right of the vast majority to run their affairs in their own interests, and defending the right of a small minority to keep the majority in bondage; in other words, it overlooks the difference between moving forwards and backwards, between putting the clock on and putting it back, between revolution and counter-revolution. Of course, if we fight to achieve socialism, and if we achieve it, then we shall defend what we have achieved and shall not allow the slightest possibility of any group destroying that achievement. Let the capitalists and their hangers-on shout about democracy "in general". If, as Lenin said, we "have the brains to analyse the situation", we shall not be deceived by them.

The "liberal" concept of "fairness" has, indeed, often served as a favourite weapon of reaction. In 1949 and again in 1950, when the fascists decided to hold a demonstration in London on May Day, the Home Secretary promptly banned the workers' May Day demonstration. If I ban one, I must ban the other, he blandly explained. How scrupulously "fair" he was!

Dialectics and Scientific Method

Understanding things in their circumstances and inter-connections is inseparable from understanding them in their movements and changes. For the real connections of things, the ways they affect each other, are manifested in their movements, in the processes of their coming into being and ceasing to be. A dialectical approach is fundamental in every kind of science. For the sciences disclose connections between things in processes of change, in which things acquire various properties and change their properties.

In the biological sciences, for example, this approach was the one adopted in the theory of evolution of living species. The fundamental idea of Darwin was that of the inter-relation of organism and environment in the processes of evolution. Whereas earlier theories had been content to describe each species separately and to regard each as having a fixed unmodifiable nature, created once for all, Darwin studied the differences and relations between species as arising in the process of evolution in which natural selection led to the survival of those forms which exemplified adaptation to the environment.

In considering how changes take place the sciences try to study not merely those properties and relations of things which are evident externally, but how the internal processes which

75

determine the external appearances of things are constituted and connected. This has been achieved in the progress of the physical sciences.

It is likewise exemplified in the biological sciences in recent researches and discoveries in the field of genetics. These are essentially concerned with the interconnections and changes which take place in the processes of multiplication of living cells and with how, in the whole process of the life of organisms in their environments, these affect the growth and form of organisms.

In this connection, incidentally, one has to characterise the work of Lysenko, which occasioned controversy in the Soviet Union, as a kind of miscarriage of dialectics.

Lysenko argued for the principle of the unity of the organism with the environment—and concluded that by placing organisms in modified environments, as well as by various kinds of grafts in the case of plants, one could so to speak force changes in their heredity. Sometimes these attempts were successful, and he argued rightly against antique theories that the hereditary nature of organisms was unchangeable. But by describing the theory of genes and of the interaction of genes as "metaphysical" (and, indeed, "idealist") he himself was guilty of an extremely undialectical and unmaterialist approach—failing to see the necessity of studying the interconnection of internal and external processes in the determination of the growth and changes of organisms.

Considering Things in their Movement

The principle of considering things in their movement, their change, their coming into being and going out of being is of paramount importance not only in the natural sciences but in the understanding of society and in revolutionary practice. Here it is necessary always to pay attention to what is new, to what is rising and growing—not just to what exists at the moment, but to what is coming into being.

The Russian Bolsheviks, for example, saw from the very beginning how Russian society was moving—what was new in it, what was coming into being. They looked for what was rising and growing, though it was still weak—the working class. While others discounted the importance of the working class and finished by entering into compromises with the forces of the old society, the Bolsheviks concluded that the working class was the new, rising force, and led it to victory.

Similarly today, when Press and radio are full of the boasts and threats of the American imperialists and their followers, we stress that which is rising and growing all over the world, the people's camp of peace, which is bound to continue to grow and to overwhelm the imperialists in shameful disaster.

Again, in the fight for unity of the working-class movement, in relation to the British Labour Party and the affiliated trade unions, we pay attention above all to that which is arising and growing in the movement. Therefore we see a great deal more than the policy of the right-wing leaders and their influence. The right wing has its basis in the past, though it is still strong. But there are arising the forces of the future, determined to fight against capitalism and war.

Similarly in relation to individual people—we should foster and build on what is coming to birth in them, what is rising and moving ahead. This is what a good secretary or organiser does.

Such examples as these show that the basis of the dialectical method, its most essential principle, is to study and understand things in their concrete interconnection and movement.

Against "Ready-made Schemes"—"Truth is Always Concrete"
Sometimes people imagine that dialectics is a preconceived scheme, into the pattern of which everything is supposed to fit. This is the very opposite of the truth about dialectics. The employment of the Marxist dialectical method does not mean that we apply a preconceived scheme and try to make everything fit into it. No, it means that we study things as they really are, in their real interconnection and movement. "The most essential thing in Marxism," Lenin wrote, "is the concrete analysis of concrete conditions" (quoted by Mao Tse-tung in *On Contradiction*).

77

This is something which Lenin insisted on again and again. Indeed, in his pamphlet *One Step Forward, Two Steps Back*, he proclaimed it as "the fundamental thesis of dialectics".

> "Genuine dialectics," Lenin wrote, proceeds "by means of a thorough, detailed analysis of a process in all its concreteness. The fundamental thesis of dialectics is: there is no such thing as abstract truth, truth is always concrete."

What did he mean by "truth is always concrete"? Just that we will not get at the truth about things, either about nature or society, by thinking up some general scheme, some abstract formula; but only by trying to work out as regards each process just what are the forces at work, how they are related, which are rising and growing and which are decaying and dying away, and on this basis reaching an estimate of the process as a whole.

So Engels said: "There could be no question of building the laws of dialectics into nature, but of discovering them in it and evolving them from it. . . . Nature is the test of dialectics" (*Anti-Dühring*).

As regards the study of society, and the estimate we make of real social changes on which we base our political strategy, Lenin ridiculed those who took some abstract, preconceived scheme as their guide.

According to some "authorities", the Marxist dialectics laid it down that all development must proceed through "triads"— thesis, antithesis, synthesis. Lenin ridiculed this.

> "It is clear to everybody that the main burden of Engels' argument is that materialists must depict the historical process correctly and accurately, and that insistence on . . . selection of examples which demonstrate the correctness of the triad is nothing but a relic of Hegelianism. . . . And, indeed, once it has been categorically declared that to attempt to 'prove' anything by triads is absurd, what significance can examples of 'dialectical' process have? . . . Anyone who reads the definition and description of the dialectical method given by Engels will see that the Hegelian

triads are not even mentioned, and that it all amounts to regarding social evolution as a natural-historical process of development. . . .

What Marx and Engels called the dialectical method is nothing more nor less than the scientific method in sociology, which consists in regarding society as a living organism in a constant state of development, the study of which requires an objective analysis of the relations of production which constitute the given social formation and an investigation of its laws of functioning and development" (*What the "Friends of the People" Are and How They Fight the Social Democrats*, Part I).

Let us consider some examples of what the "analysis of a process in all its concreteness" and the principle that "truth is always concrete" mean, in contrast to the method of trying to lay down some preconceived scheme of social development and of appealing to such a scheme as a basis for policy.

In Tsarist Russia the Mensheviks used to say: "We must have capitalism before socialism." First capitalism must go through its full development, then socialism will follow: that was their scheme. Consequently they supported the liberals in politics and enjoined the workers to do no more than fight for better conditions in the capitalist factories.

Lenin repudiated this silly scheme. He showed that the liberals, frightened by the workers, would compromise with the Tsar; but that the alliance of workers with peasants could take the lead from them, overthrow the Tsar, and then go on to overthrow the capitalists and build socialism before ever capitalism was able to develop fully.

After the proletarian revolution was successful, another scheme was propounded—this time by Trotsky. "You can't build socialism in one country. Unless the revolution takes place in the advanced capitalist countries, socialism cannot come in Russia." Lenin and Stalin showed that this scheme, too, was false. For even if the revolution did not take place in the advanced capitalist countries, the alliance of workers and peasants in the Soviet Union had still the forces to build socialism.

In Western European countries it used often to be said: "We must have fascism before communism." First the capitalists will abandon democracy and introduce the fascist dictatorship, and then the workers will overthrow the fascist dictatorship. But the Communists replied, no, we will fight together with all the democratic forces to preserve bourgeois democracy and to defeat the fascists, and that will create the best conditions for going forward to win working-class power and to commence to build socialism.

Lastly, today we sometimes hear the argument: "Capitalism means war; therefore war is inevitable." No, this scheme is false as well. The imperialists have tried to stake their policy on wars of conquest. But they cannot make war without the people. The more they prepare for war, the more open their aggressiveness becomes, the more one power attempts to impose its domination on another and the more hardships they impose on the people, the more can the people be rallied to oppose their war. Therefore peace can be preserved. And by fighting to preserve peace we can lay the basis for ending the conditions which create the danger of war. So war is not inevitable: the imperialist plans can be defeated. They can be defeated if the working class rallies all the peace-loving forces around itself. And if we defeat the imperialist war plans, that will be the best road towards the ending of capitalism itself and the building of socialism. Imperialism will not be ended by waiting for it to wreck itself in inevitable wars, but by uniting to prevent the realisation of its war plans.

In all these examples it will be seen that the acceptance of some ready-made scheme, some abstract formula, means passivity, support for capitalism, betrayal of the working class and of socialism. But the dialectical approach which understands things in their concrete interconnection and movement, shows us how to forge ahead—how to fight, what allies to draw in. That is the inestimable value of the Marxist dialectical method to the working-class movement.

Chapter Eight

THE LAWS OF DEVELOPMENT

What Do We Mean by "Development"?

When we study any processes, whether of nature or of society, we always find, as Stalin observed in *Dialectical and Historical Materialism*, that there is "renewal and development, where something is always arising and developing and something always disintegrating and dying away".

When that which is arising and developing comes to fruition, and that which is disintegrating and dying away finally disappears, there emerges something *new*.

For as we saw in criticising mechanistic materialism, processes do not always keep repeating the same cycle of changes, but advance from stage to stage as something new continually emerges.

This is the real meaning of the word "development". We speak of "development" where stage by stage something new keeps emerging.

Thus there is a difference between mere *change* and development. Development is change proceeding according to its own internal laws from stage to stage.

And there is equally a difference between *growth* and development. This difference is familiar to biologists, for example. Thus growth means getting bigger—merely quantitative change. But development means, not getting bigger, but passing into a qualitatively new stage, becoming qualitatively different.

For example, a caterpillar grows longer and fatter; then it spins itself a cocoon, and finally emerges as a butterfly. This is development. A caterpillar *grows* into a bigger caterpillar; it *develops* into a butterfly.

Processes of nature and history exemplify, not merely change, not merely growth, but development. Can we, then, reach any conclusions about the general laws of development? This is the further task of materialist dialectics—to find what general laws are manifested in all development, and to give us, therefore, the *method of approach* for understanding, explaining and controlling development.

Quantity and Quality; The Law of the Transformation of Quantitative into Qualitative Changes

This brings us to consideration of so-called "laws of dialectics", and first to what is known as "the law of the transformation of quantitative into qualitative change". What does this mean?

All change has a quantitative aspect, that is, an aspect of mere increase or decrease which does not alter the nature of that which changes.

But quantitative change, increase or decrease, cannot go on indefinitely. At a certain point it always leads to a qualitative change; and at that critical point (or "nodal point", as Hegel called it) the qualitative change takes place relatively suddenly, by a leap, as it were.

For example, if water is being heated, it does not go on getting hotter and hotter indefinitely; at a certain critical temperature, it begins to turn into steam, undergoing a qualitative change from liquid to gas. A cord used to lift a weight may have a greater and greater load attached to it, but no cord can lift a load indefinitely great: at a certain point, the cord is bound to break. A boiler may withstand a greater and greater pressure of steam—up to the point where it bursts.

This law of the transformation of quantitative into qualitative change is also met with in society. Thus before the system of industrial capitalism comes into being there takes place a process of the accumulation of wealth in money form in a few private hands (largely by colonial plunder), and of the formation of a propertyless proletariat (by enclosures and the driving of peasants off the land). At a certain point in this process, when *enough* money is accumulated to provide capital for industrial undertakings, when *enough* people have been proletarianised to provide the labour required, the conditions have matured for the development of industrial capitalism. At this point an accumulation of quantitative changes gives rise to a new qualitative stage in the development of society.

In general, qualitative changes happen with relative suddenness—by a leap. Something new is suddenly born, though its potentiality was already contained in the gradual evolutionary process of continuous quantitative change which went before.

Thus we find that continuous, gradual quantitative change leads at a certain point to discontinuous, sudden qualitative change. We have already remarked in an earlier chapter that most of those who have considered the laws of development in nature and society have conceived of this development only in its continuous aspect. This means that they have considered it only from the aspect of a process of growth, of quantitative change, and have not considered its qualitative aspect, the fact that at a certain point in the gradual process of growth a new quality suddenly arises, a transformation takes place.

Yet this is what always happens. If you are boiling a kettle, the water suddenly begins to boil when boiling point is reached. If you are scrambling eggs, the mixture in the pan suddenly "scrambles". And it is the same if you are engaged in changing society. We will only change capitalist society into socialist society when the rule of one class is replaced by the rule of another class—and this is a radical transformation, a leap to a new state of society, a revolution.

If, on the other hand, we consider quality itself, then qualitative change always arises as a result of an accumulation of quantitative changes, and differences in quality have their basis in differences of quantity.

Thus just as quantitative change must at a certain point give rise to qualitative change, so if we wish to bring about qualitative change we must study its quantitative basis, and know what must be increased and what diminished if the required chance is to be brought about.

Natural science teaches us how purely quantitative difference—addition or subtraction—makes a qualitative difference

83

in nature. For example, the addition of one proton in the nucleus of an atom makes the transition from one element to another. The atoms of all the elements are formed out of combinations of the same protons and electrons, but a purely quantitative difference between the numbers combined in the atom gives different kinds of atoms, atoms of different elements with different chemical properties. Thus an atom consisting of one proton and one electron is a hydrogen atom, but if another proton and another electron are added it is an atom of helium, and so on. Similarly in chemical compounds, the addition of one atom to a molecule makes the difference between substances with different chemical properties. In general, different qualities have their basis in quantitative difference.

As Engels put it in his *Dialectics of Nature*:

"In nature, in a manner exactly fixed for each individual case, qualitative changes can only occur by the quantitative addition or subtraction of matter or motion. . . .

All qualitative differences in nature rest on differences of chemical composition or on different quantities or forms of motion or, as is almost always the case, on both. Hence it is impossible to alter the quality of a body without addition or subtraction of matter or motion, i.e. without quantitative alteration of the body concerned."

This feature of the dialectical law connecting quality and quantity is familiar to readers of the popular literature about atomic bombs. To make a uranium bomb it is necessary to have the isotope, uranium-235; the more common isotope, uranium-238, will not do. The difference between these two is merely quantitative, a difference in atomic weight, depending on the number of neutrons present in each case. But this quantitative difference of atomic weight, 235 and 238, makes the qualitative difference between a substance with the properties required for the bomb and a substance without those properties. Further, having got a quantity of uranium-235, a certain "critical mass" of it is required before it will explode. If there is not enough, the chain reaction which constitutes the explosion will not occur; when the "critical mass" is reached, the reaction does occur.

The hydrogen bomb likewise depends on definite quantitative conditions to make it go off. The thermo-nuclear reaction which constitutes the explosion takes place only when a sufficient degree of heat is present. So this heat has to be generated, e.g. by an atomic explosion, in order to explode the hydrogen bomb.

Thus we see that quantitative changes are transformed at a certain point into qualitative changes, and qualitative differences rest on quantitative differences. This is a universal feature of development. What makes such development happen?

Development Takes Place Through the Unity and Struggle of Opposites

In general, the reason why in any particular case a quantitative change leads to a qualitative change lies in the very nature, in the content, of the particular processes involved. Therefore in each case we can, if we only know enough, explain just why a qualitative change is inevitable, and why it takes place at the point it does.

To explain this we have to study the facts of the case. We cannot invent an explanation with the aid of dialectics alone; where an understanding of dialectics helps is that it gives us the clue as to where to look. In a particular case we may not yet know how and why the change takes place. In that case we have the task of finding out, by investigating the facts of the case. For there is no mystery concealed behind the emergence of the qualitatively new.

Let us consider, for example, the case of the qualitative change which takes place when water boils.

When heat is applied to a mass of water contained in a kettle, then the effect is to increase the motion of the molecules composing the water. So long as the water remains in its liquid state, the forces of attraction between the molecules are sufficient to ensure that, though some of the surface molecules are continually escaping, the whole mass coheres together as a mass of water inside the kettle. At boiling point, however, the motion of the molecules has become sufficiently violent for large numbers of them to begin jumping clear of the mass. A qualitative change is therefore observed. The water begins to bubble and the whole mass is rapidly transformed into steam. This change evidently occurs as a result of the oppositions operating within the mass of water—the tendency of the molecules to move apart and jump free versus the forces of attraction between them. The former tendency is reinforced to the point where it overcomes the latter as a result, in this case, of the external application of heat.

Another example we have considered is that of a cord which breaks when its load becomes too great. Here again, the qualitative change takes place as a result of the opposition set up between the tensile strength of the cord and the pull of the load.

These examples prepare us for the general conclusion that wherever a process of development takes place, with the transformation in it of quantitative changes into qualitative changes, there is always present in it the struggle of opposites— of opposite tendencies, opposite forces within the things and processes concerned.

Thus the law that quantitative changes are transformed into qualitative changes, and that differences in quality are based on differences in quantity, leads us to the law of the unity and struggle of opposites.

A suggestive but incomplete formulation of this law was given by Stalin in his *Dialectical and Historical Materialism*:

"Contrary to metaphysics, dialectics holds that internal contradictions are inherent in all things and phenomena of nature, for all have their negative and positive sides, a past and a future, something dying away and something developing; and that the struggle between these opposites, the struggle between the old and the new, between that which is dying away and that which is being born, between that which is disappearing and that which is developing, constitutes the internal content of the process of development, the internal content of the transformation of quantitative changes into qualitative changes.

The dialectical method therefore holds that the process of development from the lower to the higher takes place not as a harmonious unfolding of phenomena, but as a disclosure of the contradictions inherent in things and phenomena, as a 'struggle' of opposite tendencies which operate on the basis of these contradictions."

To understand development, to understand how and why quantitative changes lead to qualitative changes, to understand how and why the transition takes place from an old qualitative state to a new qualitative state, we have to understand the contradictions inherent in each thing and process we are considering, and how a "struggle" of opposite tendencies arises on the basis of these contradictions.

We have to understand this concretely, in each case, bearing in mind Lenin's warning that "the fundamental thesis of dialectics is: truth is always concrete". We cannot deduce the laws of development in the concrete case from the general principles of dialectics: we have to discover them by actual investigation in each case. But dialectics tells us what to look for.

Dialectics of Social Development—The Contradictions of Capitalism
The dialectics of development—the unity and struggle of opposites—has been most thoroughly worked out in the Marxist science of society. Here, from the standpoint of the working-class struggle, on the basis of working-class experience, we can work out the dialectic of the contradictions of capitalism and of their development very exactly.

But the principles involved in the development of society are not opposed to but are in essence the same as those involved in the development of nature, though different in their form of manifestation in each case. Thus Engels said in *Anti-Dühring*:

"I was not in doubt that amid the welter of innumerable changes taking place in nature the same dialectical laws of

87

motion are in operation as those which in history govern the apparent fortuitousness of events."

How Marxism understands the contradictions of capitalism and their development, this crowning triumph of the dialectical method, was explained in general terms by Engels in *Socialism, Utopian and Scientific*.

The basic contradiction of capitalism is not simply the conflict of two classes, which confront one another as two external forces which come into conflict. No, it is the contradiction within the social system itself, on the basis of which the class conflict arises and operates.

Capitalism brought about:

"the concentration of the means of production in large workshops and manufactories, their transformation into means of production which were in fact social. But the social means of production and the social products were treated as if they were still, as they had been before, the means of production and the products of individuals. Hitherto, the owner of the instruments of labour had appropriated the product because it was as a rule his own product, the auxiliary labour of other persons being the exception; now, the owner of the instruments of production continued to appropriate the product, although it was no longer *his* product, but exclusively the product of *others' labour*. Thus, therefore, the products, now socially produced, were not appropriated by those who had really set the means of production in motion and really produced the products, but by the *capitalists*."

The basic contradiction of capitalism is, therefore, the contradiction between socialised production and capitalist appropriation. It is on the basis of this contradiction that the struggle between the classes develops.

"In this contradiction . . . the whole conflict of today is already present in germ. . . . The contradiction between social production and capitalist appropriation became manifest as the antagonism between proletariat and bourgeoisie."

And the contradiction can only be resolved by the victory of the working class, when the working class sets up its own dictatorship and initiates social ownership and appropriation to correspond to social production.

This example very exactly illustrates the point of what Stalin said about "struggle of opposite tendencies which operate on the basis of these contradictions". The class struggle exists and operates on the basis of the contradictions inherent in the social system itself.

It is from the struggle of opposite tendencies, opposing forces, arising on the basis of the contradictions inherent in the social system, that social transformation, the leap to a qualitatively new stage of social development, takes place.

In this way the laws of dialectical development, summarised in the principles of the transformation of quantitative into qualitative change and of the unity and struggle of opposites, are found at work in the development of society. To carry into effect the socialist transformation of society, therefore, the working class must learn to understand the social situation in the light of the laws of dialectics. Guided by that understanding, it must base the tactics and strategy of its class struggle on the concrete analysis of the actual situation at each stage of the struggle.

Chapter Nine

CONTRADICTION

Contradictions Inherent in Processes

In the last chapter we considered how qualitative change is brought about by the struggle of opposed forces. This was exemplified equally in the change of state of a body from liquid to solid or gas, and in the change of society from capitalism to socialism. In each case there are "opposite tendencies" at work, whose "struggle" eventuates in some fundamental transformation, a qualitative change.

This "struggle" is not external and accidental. It is not adequately understood if we suppose that it is a question of forces or tendencies arising quite independently the one of the other, which happen to meet, to bump up against each other and come into conflict.

No. The struggle is internal and necessary; for it arises and follows from the nature of the process as a whole. The opposite tendencies are not independent the one of the other, but are inseparably connected as parts or aspects of a single whole. And they operate and come into conflict on the basis of the contradiction inherent in the process as a whole.

Movement and change result from causes *inherent* in things and processes, from *internal* contradictions.

Thus, for example, the old mechanist conception of movement was that it only happened when one body bumped into another: there were no internal causes of movement, that is, no "self-movement", but only external causes. But on the contrary, the opposed tendencies which operate in the course of the change of state of a body operate on the basis of the contradictory unity of attractive and repulsive forces inherent in all physical phenomena.

Again, the class struggle in capitalist society arises on the basis of the contradictory unity of socialised labour and private appropriation inherent in that society. It does not arise as a result of external causes, but as a result of the contradictions within the very essence of the capitalist system. On the other hand, Tory and right-wing Labour theoreticians make out that the class struggle is stirred up by external interference— by "Communist agitators" and "Soviet agents". And they believe that if only this external interference could be stopped, the system could get along very well as it is.

The internal necessity of the struggle of opposed forces, and of its outcome, based on the contradictions inherent in the process as a whole, is no mere refinement of philosophical analysis. It is of very great practical importance.

Bourgeois theorists, for example, are well able to recognise the fact of class conflicts in capitalist society. What they do not recognise is the necessity of this conflict; that it is based on contradictions inherent in the very nature of the capitalist system and that, therefore, the struggle can only culminate in and end with the destruction of the system itself and its replacement by a new, higher system of society. So they seek to mitigate the class conflict, to tone it down and reconcile the opposing classes, or to stamp it out, and so to preserve the system intact. Precisely this bourgeois view of the class conflict is brought into the labour movement by social democracy.

It was in opposition to such a shallow, metaphysical way of understanding class conflict that Lenin pointed out in *The State and Revolution*:

"It is often said and written that the core of Marx's theory is the class struggle; but it is not true. . . . To limit Marxism to the theory of the class struggle means curtailing Marxism, distorting it, reducing it to something which is acceptable to the bourgeoisie. A Marxist is one who extends the acceptance of the class struggle to the acceptance of the dictatorship of the proletariat. This is where the profound difference lies between a Marxist and an ordinary petty (or even big) bourgeois. This is the touchstone on which the real understanding and acceptance of Marxism should be tested."

In general, contradiction is inherent in a given process. The struggle which is characteristic of the process is not an external clash of accidentally opposed factors, but is the working out of contradictions belonging to the very nature of the process. And this conditions the outcome of the process.

Contradiction Consists of the Unity and Struggle of Opposites

The key conception of dialectics is this conception of contradiction inherent in the very nature of things—that the motive force of qualitative change lies in the contradictions contained within all processes of nature and society, and that in order to understand, control and master things in practice we must proceed from the concrete analysis of their contradictions.

What exactly do we mean by "contradiction"?

According to the common, metaphysical conception, contradictions occur in our ideas about things, but not in things. We can assert contradictory propositions about a thing, and then there is a contradiction in what we say about it; but there can be no contradiction in the thing. This point of view regards contradiction simply and solely as a logical relation between propositions, but does not consider it as a real relation between things. Such a point of view is based on considering things statically, as "fixed and frozen", disregarding their motions and dynamic interconnections.

If we consider the real, complex movements and interconnections of real, complex things, then we find that contradictory tendencies can and do exist in them. For example, if the forces operating in a body combine tendencies of attraction and of repulsion, that it is a real contradiction. And if the movement of society combines the tendency to socialise production with the tendency to preserve private appropriation of the products, that is a real contradiction too.

The existence of contradictions in things is a very familiar state of affairs. There is nothing in the least abstruse about it, and it is often referred to in everyday conversations. For example, we speak of a man as having a "contradictory" character, or as being "a mass of contradictions". This means that he evinces opposed tendencies in his behaviour, such as gentleness and brutality, recklessness and cowardice, selfishness and self-sacrifice. Or again, contradictory relations are the subject of everyday gossip when we talk about married couples who are always quarrelling but never happy apart.

Such examples show that when we speak in Marxist philosophy about "contradictions in things", we are not inventing some far-fetched philosophical theory, but are referring to something which is familiar to everyone. Nor are we using the word "contradiction" in some new and strange sense of our own, but are using the word in its ordinary, everyday sense.

A real contradiction is a *unity* of opposites. There is a real contradiction inherent, as we say, in the very nature of a thing or process or relationship when in that thing or process or relationship opposite tendencies are combined together in such a way that neither can exist without the other. In the unity of opposites, the opposites are held together in a relation of mutual dependence, where each is the condition of existence of the other.

For example, the class contradiction between workers and capitalists in capitalist society is just such a unity of opposites, because in that society neither can the workers exist without the capitalists nor the capitalists without the workers. The nature of the society is such that these opposites are held together in it in inseparable unity. This unity of opposites belongs to the very essence of the social system. Capitalism is a system in which capitalists exploit workers and workers are exploited by capitalists.

It is the unity of opposites in a contradiction which makes inescapable and necessary the *struggle* of opposites. Since the opposed terms are inseparably united, there is no getting out of the struggle. Thus, for example, because opposed classes are united in capitalist society, the development of that society

93

proceeds, and cannot but proceed, in the form of a class struggle.

We may also speak of the *interpenetration* of opposites in a contradiction. For being united in struggle, each opposed tendency is in its actual character and operation at any phase of the struggle influenced, modified or penetrated by the other in many ways. Each side is always affected by its relation with the other.

The Working Out of Contradictions

We can only understand, and can only control and master, the processes of nature and of society by understanding their contradictions, and the consequences of those contradictions—the way they work out.

Contradiction is the driving force of change. So if we want to understand how things change, and to control and utilise their changes, then we must understand their contradictions.

Why should we say that contradiction is the driving force of change? It is because it is only the presence of contradictions in a process which provides the internal conditions making change necessary. A process which contained no contradictions would simply go on and on in the same way until some external force stopped it or modified it. A movement without contradictions would be continuous repetition of the same movement. It is the presence of contradictions, that is, of contradictory tendencies of movement, or of a unity and struggle of opposites, which brings about *changes* of movement in the course of a process.

Imagine, if you can, a society without contradictions. This would be a society in which by continuing to do the same things in the same ways people would satisfy all their needs. Such a society would never change. There would continually be movement in it, in as much as people would be doing things all the time; but the movement would always be the same. There would be a process, but a process of repetition.

However, no such society exists or ever could exist, because from the very nature of the conditions of human life there must

94

always be contradictions in society. By satisfying their needs people create new unsatisfied needs, and by advancing their forces of production they bring about a state of affairs in which they need to change their social relations and institutions correspondingly. This is why changes happen in society. The social process is not a process of repetition but a process in which new things happen.

Again, some metaphysical materialists tried to represent the universe as a system of particles bumping into and bouncing off one another. Such a universe would be a universe of the continuous motion of particles, but it would be a universe of the continuous repetition of the same motion. The real universe is not like this, because it is full of contradictions— the contradictions of attraction and repulsion studied by physics, of the association and dissociation of atoms studied by chemistry, of the processes of life and of the relationship of organism with environment studied by biology. It is the working out of these contradictions (in their specific forms in specific processes) which makes up the real changing processes of the real changing world.

This shows that where contradictions exist, there follows the working out of those contradictions—the working out of the struggle of opposites which arises from the unity of opposites. A process is the working out of its own essential contradictions.

The Universality and Particularity of Contradictions
Contradiction is a universal feature of all processes. But each particular kind of process has its own particular contradictions, which are characteristic of it and different from those of other processes.

This point was underlined by Mao Tse-tung in his essay *On Contradiction*, which remains one of the most suggestive analyses of the conception yet contributed to Marxist literature. He called it the distinction between "the universality" and "the particularity" of contradiction.

We can never deduce what will happen in any particular case, or how a particular process can be controlled, from the

95

universal idea of contradiction. As has already been stressed, the dialectical method does not consist in applying some pre-conceived scheme to the interpretation of everything, but consists in basing conclusions only on the "concrete analysis of concrete conditions".

Each kind of process has its own dialectic, which can be grasped only by the detailed study of that particular process. The dialectic of the sub-atomic world is not the same as that of the bodies directly perceptible to our senses. The dialectic of living organisms is not the same as that of the processes of inorganic matter. The dialectic of human society is a new law of motion. And each phase of human society brings with it again its own particular dialectic.

Thus, for example, the contradiction between tendencies of attraction and repulsion in physical motion, and between the interests of classes in society, are both contradictions. This is evidence of the universality of contradiction. But each has its own distinctive character, different from that of the other. This is evidence of the particularity of contradiction.

We cannot learn either the laws of physics or the laws of society if we try to deduce them from the universal idea of contradiction. We can learn them only by investigating physical and social processes. Physical movements and the movement of people in society are quite different forms of movement, and so the contradictions studied by social science are different, and work out in a different way, from those studied by physics. Social and physical processes are similar in that each contains contradictions, but dissimilar in the contradictions each contains.

The contradictions characteristic of each kind of process may be called the essential contradictions of that kind of process. For instance, contradictions between attractive and repulsive forces are essential contradictions of physical pro-cesses, and contradictions between forces of production and relations of production are essential contradictions of social processes.

If we further consider the essential contradictions character-istic of different kinds of process, then we can further say that these are manifested in specific ways in specific instances of processes of a given kind.

For example, the essential contradictions of social processes are manifested in specific ways in each specific social formation. The contradiction between forces of production and relations of production takes specific forms in different formations of society. Thus in capitalist society it takes the specific capitalist form of the contradiction between the increasingly social character of production and the retention of private appropriation.

Again, the relations between any species of living organism and its environment are contradictory. The organism lives only by means of its environment, and at the same time its environment contains threats to its life which it has continually to overcome. In the case of man, this contradiction takes the form of the specific contradictory relation between man and nature; and this relation itself takes even more specific forms with each stage of man's social development. Man is a part of nature and lives by means of nature, and man lives by opposing himself to nature and subduing nature to his will. This contradictory relation itself develops, and takes specific forms, as man develops. It is present in both primitive communism and in communism, for example, but presents a different aspect in the latter from the former.

In order to understand a process, then, and to learn how to control and master it, we must get to know its essential contradictions and investigate the specific forms they take in specific instances.

The Outcome of Contradictions

The unity of opposites in a contradiction is characterised by a definite relation of superiority-inferiority, or of domination, between the opposites. For example, in a physical unity of attraction and repulsion, certain elements of attraction or repulsion may be dominant in relation to others. The unity is such that one side dominates the other—or, in certain cases, they may be equal.

Any qualitative state of a process corresponds to a definite relation of domination. Thus, the solid, liquid and gaseous states of bodies correspond to different domination-relationships in the unity of attraction and repulsion characteristic of the molecules of bodies. Similarly, in the contradictions of capitalist society, the element of private appropriation plays a dominant rôle in relation to its opposite, social production, and the capitalist class dominates over the working class. If these domination relationships become reversed, then that marks a qualitative change, the ending of the capitalist state of society, the beginning of a new state.

Domination relationships are obviously, by their very nature, impermanent and apt to change, even though in some cases they remain unchanged for a long time. If the relationship takes the form of equality or balance, such balance is by nature unstable, for there is a struggle of opposites within it which is apt to lead to the domination of one over the other. And then if one dominates over the other, the struggle of opposites contains the possibility of the position being reversed.

"The unity of opposites," said Lenin, "is conditional, temporary, transitory, relative. The struggle of opposites is absolute." That is obviously true. Whatever the domination relationship in the unity of opposites may be, it is always apt to change, as a result of which the former unity of opposites will be dissolved and a new unity of opposites take its place.

The outcome of the working out of contradictions is, then, a change in the domination relation characteristic of the initial unity of opposites. Such a change constitutes a change in the nature of a thing, a change from one state to another, a change from one thing to another, a change entailing not merely some external alteration but a change in the internal character and laws of motion of a thing.

It is precisely such a change that we mean by a "qualitative" change.

For instance, if a piece of iron is painted black and instead we paint it red, that is merely an external alteration (affecting the way it reflects light and so its appearance to a seeing eye), but it is not a qualitative change in the sense we are here defining. On the other hand, if the iron is heated to melting point, then this *is* such a qualitative change. And it comes about precisely as a change in the attraction-repulsion relationship characteristic of the internal molecular state of the metal. The metal passes from the solid to liquid state, its internal character and laws of motion become different in certain ways, it undergoes a qualitative change.

Qualitative change is the result of a change in the balance of opposites. Such a change is prepared by a series of quantitative changes affecting the domination relation in the unity of opposites. As the domination relation changes, quantitative change passes into qualitative change.

When such a fundamental or qualitative change comes about as a result of the dissolution of an old form of unity of opposites and the coming into being of a new one, then the opposites themselves change. The side which passes from being dominated over to being dominant is changed in that process, and so is the other side, which passes from being dominant to being dominated over. Hence in the new qualitative state there are not the same old opposites in a changed relation, but because the relation is changed the opposites, held together in that relation, are changed too. There is a new unity of opposites, a new contradiction.

When, for instance, the working class becomes stronger than the capitalist class and from being dominated over becomes dominant, then in the new qualitative state of society the capitalist class disappears (for the dominant working class deprives it of its conditions of existence), and the working class, existing in completely new conditions, becomes virtually a new class. The contradictions of society therefore change; the particular contradictions of the old state disappear and new contradictions are born. The struggle between the working class and the capitalists comes to an end, and new kinds of struggle begin.

External and Internal Causes of Qualitative Change
How far is the passage from quantitative to qualitative change determined by the working out of the contradiction inherent

in the process itself, or by internal causes, and how far is it determined by external or accidental causes?

It is determined by both, but in different ways.

Both in nature and society different things are always interacting and influencing each other. Hence external causes must always play a part in the changes which happen to things. At the same time, the character of the changes always depends on internal causes.

This problem was discussed by Mao Tse-tung in his essay *On Contradiction*. He concluded:

> "Contradiction within a thing is the basic cause of its development, while the relationship of a thing with other things—their interconnection and interaction—is a secondary cause. . . . External causes are the condition of change and internal causes the basis of change, external causes becoming operative through internal causes."

Consider, for example, such an event as the hatching of a chicken. The chicken does not develop inside the egg unless heat is applied from outside. But what develops in the egg, what hatches out, depends on what is inside the egg. As Mao remarks: "In a suitable temperature an egg changes into a chicken, but there is no temperature which can change a stone into a chicken, the fundamentals of the two things being different."

Again, water does not boil unless it is heated. But the boiling process resulting from the application of heat comes about on the basis of the internal contradiction of attraction and repulsion characteristic of the molecules of water.

Similarly in society, a revolution does not proceed without the intervention of external causes, but its character and outcome, and indeed the fact that it happens at all, depend on internal causes. Thus the basis of the Russian Revolution lay in the contradictions within Russian society. These made the revolution inevitable and determined its character. But what actually set off the revolution in 1917 was something external, the conditions brought about by the imperialist war.

In general, if we consider qualitative changes, then their qualitative character can be explained only by the operation of internal causes; the particular contradictions on which the old quality was based determine what new quality emerges. The external causes affect only the quantitative changes of things—the times and places of their beginning, and the rate at which they proceed.

"Purely external causes can only lead . . . to changes in size and quantity, but cannot explain why things are qualitatively different in a thousand and one ways and why things change into one another" (Mao Tse-tung, *On Contradiction*).

Thus, for example, the class struggle in capitalist society may be speeded up or slowed down by a variety of particular external causes. But the existence of the class struggle, its continuation, its direction and its final outcome are determined by the contradictions inherent in the capitalist system.

The Suddenness and Gradualness of Qualitative Change

Qualitative change being the outcome of the working out of contradictions, it follows that the whole process of the struggle of opposites may be regarded as a process of the replacement of one quality by another, of an old quality by a new one. The old quality corresponds to the dominance of one element in the unity of opposites. The reversal of this dominance leads to the replacement of the old quality by the new. In this sense each element in a unity of opposites is the bearer of a distinct quality. The struggle of the one to maintain its dominance is what maintains the old quality, the struggle of the other to reverse this dominance is what brings into being the new quality replacing the old.

For instance, all life is a unity of opposites, of processes of the building up and breaking down of living matter. So long as the building up maintains itself within this unity, life remains. When, however, the opposite begins to dominate, then death commences.

Again, if we consider the contradictions of capitalist society, then it is evident that the capitalist state of society depends on private appropriation dominating social production, and the capitalist class dominating the working class. It is the struggle of the working class against the capitalist class, and the struggle to free social production from the fetters of private appropriation, which, when the reversal of the old state happens, brings about a new socialist state of society.

It has already been pointed out that every contradiction has its own specific character. And so the struggle of opposites has in every case also its own specific character, according to the particular contradiction from which it arises. It follows that processes of qualitative change, replacements of old by new qualities, have also each their own specific character, according to the qualities concerned. What is *universally* true is simply that qualitative change comes about as the working out of contradictions, as an outcome of quantitative change. But this universal truth does not tell us how any *particular* change will work out. We can only discover that by knowing each particular case.

Thus considering the workings out of different kinds of social contradictions, which result in qualitative changes in society, each works out differently. For example, the contradiction between the great mass of the people and the feudal lords was worked out in the struggle for the democratic revolution; that between the working class and the capitalist class is worked out in the struggle for socialist revolution; that between the colonies and imperialism is worked out in the national liberation struggle; and that between the working class and peasantry in socialist society, in the collectivisation and mechanisation of agriculture.

Whatever the method by which different contradictions work out, a point is always reached where the quantitative aspect of the struggle of opposites within the contradiction has been sufficiently modified for the new quality to emerge. This is the point where qualitative change *begins*. How it *continues* depends entirely on the particular character of the contradiction of which it is the outcome, on the particular way the struggle of opposites continues.

Qualitative change is always sudden, and cannot but be sudden, in the sense that at a certain point of quantitative change a new quality emerges which was not present before. That is to say, at this point new things begin to happen, new causes operate and new effects are produced, new laws of motion come into operation.

This is the so-called qualitative "leap", the first appearance of the new which was not there before.

Thus qualitative change is preceded by a process of working up to the emergence of new quality. During this process contradictions are working out, so to speak, unseen—without manifestation in qualitative change. At the termination of this phase, the phase of the emergence of new quality begins abruptly or suddenly, and cannot but do so.

For example, when water is heated a movement takes place which suddenly turns into a boiling process. When a child is growing in the womb a movement takes place which suddenly turns into the process of birth. In society movement takes place amongst the classes, conflicts are sharpened, opinions mature, and suddenly there begins a decisive revolutionary change.

After that, how qualitative change proceeds, the swiftness or slowness and, in general, the manner of its completion, depends entirely on the circumstances of particular cases. Once a new quality emerges—once it has leaped into being—then a process of new qualitative character beings, in which the new quality gradually supplants the old.

While, therefore, qualitative change begins suddenly, it continues gradually. How quickly or how slowly the new supplants the old depends on the nature of the process and the conditions under which it occurs.

For instance, physical changes of state, such as water coming to the boil, are sudden, because a point is suddenly reached when a new thing, steam, begins to be formed: but the conversion of water into steam is a gradual process. It is the same with chemical changes. And it is the same again with qualitative changes in society. A point is reached in the working out of social contradictions where the qualitative change begins—the change from the power of one class to the power of another class, from one system of production relations to another: after that, this change may take a longer or shorter time to be completed.

Take, for example, the political aspect of social revolutions, that is, the conquest of state power. In the Russian socialist revolution this took place by a single blow—which means, comparatively quickly. In a few days all the decisive positions of power passed into the hands of the working class. In the next round of socialist revolutions—those in the present people's democracies—it took place over a longer period, by a series of steps in which first one and then another position of power was conquered. If we look back to the revolutions through which the bourgeoisie formerly won power from the feudal lords, then these took place over a longer period still— often extending over many years.

Or if we consider economic changes, these tend to be comparatively slow, taking place through a series of steps. For instance, capitalist relations, once they emerged in feudal society, extended their scope step by step over a long period. Again, the displacement of capitalism by socialism, once begun, is another gradual process, though it takes place more rapidly than the displacement of feudalism by capitalism. (It takes place more rapidly for a definite reason, namely, that socialism cannot begin to displace capitalism until after the working class has won state power, and then the power of the state operates to direct and speed up economic change. The change from feudalism to capitalism, on the other hand, generally begins long before state power passes into the hands of the capitalist class, and meanwhile the feudal state acts rather to slow down than to speed up the change.)

These examples show that there is a quantitative side to qualitative change, namely, the power and speed with which it completes itself. And naturally, under certain unfavourable circumstances it may never be completed at all. In certain cases it is possible for the change to begin, and then be turned back again and disappear.

The dialectical materialist conception of contradiction includes both the suddenness and gradualness of qualitative change. The difference between this conception of change and that of many other philosophies is not that dialectical materialism lays it down that all qualitative changes are sudden, whereas the others say they are gradual. It is that dialectical materialism understands change as coming from the struggle of opposites, from the working out of contradictions, whereas the others overlook or deny this. They suppose that change comes in a smooth way, without conflicts, or else by merely external conflicts.

Antagonism and Non-antagonism in Contradictions
The working out of contradictions always involves one side struggling with and overcoming the other. But according to the nature of the contradiction, this process may take place in different ways. And in society in particular, a distinction must be drawn between contradictions the solution of which involves the forcible suppression or destruction of one side by the other, and those whose solution does not require such methods.

The change from capitalism to socialism, for example, takes place through the forcible suppression of the capitalist class by the working class. But the ensuing change from socialism to communism does not require the forcible suppression of anyone. The former change is effected by means of a struggle between mutually antagonistic forces, whereas no such antagonisms have to be fought out to effect the latter change.

In general, social contradictions are antagonistic when they involve conflicts of economic interest. In such cases one group imposes its own interests on another, and one group suppresses another by forcible methods. But when conflicts of economic interest are not involved, there is no antagonism and therefore no need for the forcible suppression of any group by any other. Once class antagonisms are done away with in socialist society, all social questions can be settled by discussion and argument, by criticism and self-criticism, by persuasion, conviction and agreement.

Antagonism, therefore, is not the same thing as contradiction. Nor is it the same thing as the struggle of opposites within a contradiction. The struggle of opposites is a universal, necessary feature of every contradiction, and it may take an antagonistic form or it may not, depending on the particular nature of the particular contradiction.

So Lenin remarked that "antagonism and contradiction are utterly different. Under socialism antagonism disappears, but contradiction remains" (*Critical Notes on Bukharin's "Economics of the Transition Period"*).

As Mao Tse-tung put it: "Antagonism is only one form of struggle within a contradiction, but not its universal form."

The distinction between antagonism and non-antagonism in the contradictions of society is of great practical importance. There are many contradictions in society, and it is practically important to distinguish which are antagonistic and which are not, in order to find the right method of dealing with them. If a contradiction of the one kind is mistaken for a contradiction of the other kind, then wrong action is taken which cannot lead to the desired results.

For example, reformist socialists think there is no need for the working class to take power and use it to suppress the capitalist class, whereas Marxists recognise that capitalism can be ended and socialism achieved by no other method. But when socialism is established classes and class antagonisms disappear, and so methods of struggle right for the fighting out of class antagonisms are wrong for the ensuing struggle to pass from socialism to communism. Contradictions remain, but since they no longer take the form of antagonism of interest they do not require for their solution forcible measures to impose the interests of one section upon another.

The distinction between antagonism and non-antagonism in contradictions within society is a distinction between those contradictions which can work out only by the use of material force by one side against the other, and those which can work out entirely as a result of discussions among the members of society and agreed decisions taken after such discussion. Contradictions of this last kind are a special kind of contradiction which can arise only among rational human beings, and among them only when they are united in co-operation for a common interest and not divided by antagonistic interests. In such contradictions there appears the new element of the rational, purposive, consciously controlled working out of contradictions, as opposed to the blind working out of contradictions in nature—the new element of human freedom as opposed to natural necessity.

When all means of production are brought fully under planned social direction, then it may be expected that men's mastery over nature will enormously increase, and the conquest and transformation of nature by man will in turn mean profound changes in men's mode of life. For instance, ability to produce an absolute abundance of products with a minimum expenditure of labour, and abolition of the antithesis between manual and intellectual labour clearly imply profound changes in social organisation, in outlook, in habits, in mode of life generally. The effecting of such changes cannot but involve, at each stage, the overcoming of forms of social organisation, of outlooks and habits, belonging to the past. Development, therefore, will continue to take place through the disclosure of contradictions, the struggle between the new and the old. New needs and new tendencies will arise out of the existing conditions at each stage, which will come into contradiction with the existing forms of social organisation and social life, and hence lead to their passing and giving way to new forms. But there is no reason to expect that this development will take place, as hitherto, through violent conflicts and social upheavals. On the contrary, when men understand the laws of their own social organisation and have it under their own co-operative control, then it is possible to do away with old conditions and create new conditions in an agreed and planned way, without violent conflict or upheaval. Contradiction and the overcoming of the old by the new remains; but the element of antagonism and conflict between men in society disappears and gives way to the properly human method of deciding affairs—by scientific appraisal of conditions, needs and courses of action.

Chapter Ten

DEVELOPMENT AND NEGATION

The Forward Movement of Development
In many processes the working out of their contradictions results in a directed or forward movement, in which the process moves forward from stage to stage, each stage being an advance to something new, not a falling back to some stage already past.

Other processes, however, are not characterised by such a forward movement.

For instance, water when cooled or heated undergoes a qualitative change, passes into a new state (ice or steam), but the movement is without direction and cannot be called either progressive or retrogressive. If, for example, we are making tea, then we might call it a move forward to turn water into steam; if we are making iced drinks, then ice is a move forward. The fact is that ice can turn into water and water into steam, and back again, and this movement has no direction of its own. When, however, we consider such a movement as that of society, we find that it has a direction of its own: society moves forward from primitive communism to slavery, from slavery to feudalism, from feudalism to capitalism, from capitalism to communism. This is a movement with a direction, a "forward" movement.

Hegel used to think that natural processes were all of the undirected kind (like ice-water-steam-water-ice), and that a direction could only come into processes when "spirit" or "consciousness" was at work in them.

"The changes that take place in nature," he wrote in the Introduction to his *Philosophy of History*, "however infinitely various they may be, exhibit only a perpetually repeating cycle; in nature there takes place 'nothing new under the sun' . . . only in those changes which take place in the region of Spirit does anything new arise."

But the distinction does not in fact depend on any difference between "nature" and "spirit". A movement can have a direction without any consciousness being present to direct it. Spirit or consciousness itself is a product of nature; biological changes, leading up to man, have a direction; so have geological changes; so have processes in the evolution of stars; and so on. In general, direction in processes has a "natural" explanation. If some processes have direction and others have not, this depends solely on the particular character of the processes themselves and of the conditions under which they happen.

In general, since qualitative change in a process is always consequent upon quantitative change, it has a direction when those quantitative changes arise from conditions permanently operating within the process itself, and otherwise it has no direction. It has a direction when (however conditioned by external factors) it is impelled forward by internal causes. In that case the direction it takes is "its own" just because it arises from internal causes.

What, then, is the basis of direction in processes, of the internal causes of a forward movement of development? It is to be found in the existence and long-term operation in those processes of essential contradictions which work out by taking a series of specific forms. This is what gives rise to a directed series of stages, a long-term process of development in a definite direction.

Thus, for example, if social development has a direction this arises because man exists in a permanent contradictory relationship with nature. The permanent existence of this contradiction gives rise to a permanent tendency of man to improve his forces of production, and as this tendency operates so stage by stage contradictions arise between the social forces of production and the relations of production. The direction of man's social evolution is the direction of man's mastery over nature, and the movement of society takes this direction simply because of the natural conditions of human life, the impulses to change and development which people experience because of the necessity to satisfy their needs.

Similarly, if such things as stars pass through a series of evolutionary stages, this is because the contradictory conditions of their existence give rise to continuous processes, such as radiation, the continuation of which brings about a series of qualitative stages in their history.

We certainly should not say, as some philosophers have said, that throughout infinite time the infinite universe develops from stage to stage in a predetermined direction. There is no evidence for any such assertion—indeed, there is no sense in it. We cannot speak about the direction taken by everything, but only about the direction of the development of particular things in which we are interested. The directed development of things is not due to God or Spirit working in them, nor is it the manifestation of some mysterious cosmic law, but it arises and flows from the particular contradictions of particular things. Particular things are characterised by particular contradictions, as a result of which their movement takes a particular direction.

The Contradiction between Old and New, Past and Future
When there is a forward movement of development in a process, then stage by stage there occurs a transition from an old qualitative state to a new qualitative state, the supplanting of an old quality by a new one.

The new stage of development comes into being from the working out of the contradiction inherent in the old. And the new stage itself contains a new contradiction, since it comes into being containing something of the past from which it springs and of the future to which it leads. It has, therefore, its "negative and positive sides, a past and a future, something dying away and something developing". On this basis there once again arises within it "the struggle between the old and the new, between that which is dying away and that which is being born, between that which is disappearing and that which is developing".

Thus the forward movement of development is the continuous working out of a series of contradictions. Development continually drives forward to new development. The whole process at each stage is in essence the struggle between the old and the new, that which is dying and that which is being born.

To understand the laws of development of anything we must therefore understand its contradictions and how they work out.

A process usually contains not one but many contradictions. It is a knot of contradictions. And so to understand the course of a process we must take into account all its contradictions and understand their inter-relationship.

This generally means, first of all, that we must grasp the *basic* contradiction of a process, in its general character and in the specific form it takes at each stage. The basic contradiction is that contradiction inherent in the very nature of the process which determines its direction.

Thus in society, for instance, the basic contradiction is that between the forces of production and the relations of production, and this takes a specific form at each stage of society. In capitalist society it is the contradiction between social production and private appropriation. This basic contradiction is what determines the direction of development, namely, from capitalism to socialism—to social appropriation to match social production.

Given the basic contradiction, then a process is characterised by a number of big and small consequential contradictions, the character and effects of which are conditioned by the basic contradiction. The operation and working out of these constitutes the total process of the working out of the basic contradiction towards the emergence of a new stage of the process, a new quality.

The basic contradiction works out by the instrumentality of all the struggle arising from all the consequential contradictions. In this, however, one particular contradiction generally plays the key or *principal* rôle. In other words, of all the elements, tendencies or forces entering into various forms of struggle in a knot of contradictions, there is generally one which plays the *principal* rôle in working out the basic contradiction to its solution in the realisation of a new stage and the supplanting of an old quality by a new one.

Within any capitalist country, for example, there are many contradictions. Besides the contradiction between the working class and the capitalist class, there are other contradictions between other classes—the urban petty bourgeoisie, the peasants, the landlords, etc.—as well as contradictions within the capitalist class itself. There are also contradictions of an international kind, such as those between a given capitalist country and others, and between imperialists and colonial peoples. But within all this knot of contradictions, it is the struggle of the working class with the capitalist class which, in the given country, plays the key or principal rôle in carrying society forward from capitalism to socialism. For this is the one contradiction which can work out in such a change from the dominance of one side to that of the other as will bring about a fundamental change in the quality of the whole.

Thus, for example, the contradiction between the big capitalists and the petty bourgeoisie always takes the form of domination by the big capitalists, who keep on growing stronger in relation to the petty bourgeoisie who, for their part, keep on being pressed back and growing weaker. Hence the petty bourgeoisie cannot be the principal revolutionary force in a capitalist country, and their contradiction with the big capitalists cannot be the principal contradiction. The working class, on the other hand, grows stronger as capitalism develops, and is the force which, dominated over by the capitalists, can eventually overthrow this domination. That is why the working class is the principal revolutionary force, and why the contradiction between this class and the capitalists is the principal contradiction.

To understand the laws of development of a process, therefore, one must not only understand the basic contradiction of the process at each stage, but also what is the principal force for working out the basic contradiction and carrying the process forward to the next stage.

Mao Tse-tung pointed out that "in studying any process . . . we must do our utmost to discover its principal contradiction". This may be a complex task, since what is the principal contradiction in certain circumstances may not be so in others. But unless we grasp the principal contradiction we "cannot find the crux of a problem and naturally cannot find the method of solving contradictions".

"This is the method Marx taught us when he studied capitalist society," wrote Mao. Some of the controversy now raging round some of "the Thoughts of Chairman Mao" turns on the question of finding the principal contradiction at the present stage of world social development. Mao has asserted that it is the one between imperialism and national liberation movements.

The Rôle of Negation in Development

The forward movement of development, complex as it may be in each particular case, always takes place through the struggle of the new and the old and the overcoming of the old and dying by the new and rising.

Thus in social development, in the transition from capitalism to socialism, what is new and rising in the economic life of capitalist society—social production—contradicts what is old and carried over from the past—private appropriation, and a new force arises, the working class, whose struggle against the capitalist class is a struggle for the realisation of the new stage against the defenders of the old.

This dialectical conception of development is opposed to the older liberal conception favoured by bourgeois theoreticians. The liberals recognise development and assert that progress is a universal law of nature and society. But they see it as a smooth process; and, if they have at times to recognise the existence of struggle, they see it mainly as an unfortunate interruption, more likely to impede development than to help it forward. For them, what exists has not to be supplanted by what is coming into existence, the old has not to be overcome by the new, but it has to be preserved, so that it can gradually improve itself and become a higher existence.

True to this philosophy, which they took over from the capitalists, the social democrats strove to preserve capitalism, with the idea that it could grow into socialism. And thus striving to preserve capitalism, they ended by fighting not for socialism but against it. These exponents of no struggle and class collaboration cannot avoid struggle: they simply enter into it on the other side.

Comparing the dialectical materialist, or revolutionary, conception of development with this liberal, reformist conception, we may say that the one recognises and embraces, while the other fails to recognise and shrinks from, the rôle of *negation* in development. Dialectics teaches us to understand that the new must struggle with and overcome the old, that the old must give way to and be supplanted by the new—in other words, that the old must be negated by the new.

The liberal, who thinks metaphysically, understands negation simply as saying: "No". To him negation is merely the end to something. Far from meaning advance, it means retreat; far from meaning gain, it means loss. Dialectics, on the other hand, teaches us not to be afraid of negation, but to understand how it becomes a condition of progress, a means to positive advance.

The Positive Character of Negation

"Negation in dialectics does not mean simply saying no," wrote Engels in *Anti-Dühring*.

When in the process of development the old stage is negated by the new, then, in the first place, that new stage could not have come about except as arising from and in opposition to the old. The conditions for the existence of the new arose and matured within the old. The negation is a positive advance, brought about only by the development of that which is negated. The old is not simply abolished, leaving things as though it had never existed: it is abolished only after it has itself given rise to the conditions for the new stage of advance.

In the second place, the old stage, which is negated, itself constitutes a stage of advance in the forward-moving process of development as a whole. It is negated, but the advance which took place in it is not negated. On the contrary, this advance is carried forward to the new stage, which takes into itself and carries forward all the past achievement.

For example: socialism replaces capitalism—it negates it. But the conditions for the rise and victory of socialism were born of capitalism, and socialism comes into existence as the next stage of social development after capitalism. Every achievement, every advance in the forces of production, and likewise every cultural achievement, which took place under capitalism, is not destroyed when capitalism is destroyed, but, on the contrary, is preserved and carried further.

This positive content of negation is not understood by liberals, for whom negation is "simply saying no". Moreover, they think of negation as coming only from outside, externally. Something is developing very well, and then something else comes from outside and negates it—destroys it. That is their conception. That something by its own development leads to its own negation, and thereby to a higher stage of development, lies outside their comprehension.

Thus the liberals conceive of social revolution not only as a catastrophe, as an end to ordered progress, but they believe that such a catastrophe can be brought about only by outside forces. If a revolution threatens to upset the capitalist system, that is not because of the development of the contradictions of that system itself, but is due to "agitators".

Of course, there *is* negation which takes the form simply of a blow from outside which destroys something. For instance, if I am walking along the road and am knocked down by a car, I suffer negation of a purely negative sort. Such occurrences are frequent both in nature and in society. But this is not how we must understand negation if we are to understand the *positive* rôle of negation in the process of development.

At each stage in the process of development there arises the struggle of the new with the old. The new arises and grows strong within the old conditions, and when it is strong enough it overcomes and destroys the old. This is the negation of the past stage of development, of the old qualitative state; and it means the coming into being of the new and higher stage of development, the new qualitative state.

Negation of Negation
This brings us to a further dialectical feature of development —the negation of negation.

According to the liberal idea that negation "means simply saying no", if the negation is negated then the original position is restored once more without change. According to this idea, negation is simply a negative, a taking away. Hence if the negation, the taking away, is itself negated, that merely means putting back again what was taken away. If a thief takes my watch, and then I take it away from him, we are back where we started—I have the watch again. Similarly, if I say, "It's going to be a fine day", and you say, "No, it's going to be a wet day", to which I reply, "No, it's not going to be a wet day", I have simply, by negating your negation, re-stated my original proposition.

This is enshrined in the principle of formal logic, "not not-A equals A". According to this principle, negation of negation is a fruitless proceeding. It just takes you back where you started.

Let us, however, consider a real process of development and the dialectical negation which takes place in it.

Society develops from primitive communism to the slave system. The next stage is feudalism. The next stage is capitalism. Each stage arises from the previous one, and negates it. So far we have simply a succession of stages, each following as the negation of the other and constituting a higher stage of development. But what comes next? Communism. Here there is a return to the beginning, but at a higher level of development. In place of primitive communism, based on extremely primitive forces of production, comes communism based on extremely advanced forces of production and containing within itself tremendous new potentialities of development. The old, primitive classless society has become the new and higher classless society. It has been raised, as it were, to a higher power, has reappeared on a higher level. But this has happened only because the old classless society was negated by the appearance of classes and the development of class society, and because finally class society, when it had gone through its whole development, was itself negated by the working class taking power, ending exploitation of man by man, and establishing a new classless society on the foundation of all the achievements of the whole previous development.

This is the negation of negation. But it does not take us back to the original starting point. It takes us forward to a new starting point, which is the original one raised, through its negation and the negation of the negation, to a higher level.

Thus we see that in the course of development, as a result of a double negation, a later stage can repeat an earlier stage, but repeat it on a higher level of development.

The importance of this conception of negation of negation does not lie in its supposedly expressing the necessary pattern of all development. All development takes place through the working out of contradictions—that is a necessary universal law; but specific contradictions do not necessarily work out in such a way that an earlier stage of development is repeated at a later stage—sometimes that may happen and sometimes not, depending on the specific character of the processes of development.

Yet the repetition of an earlier stage *is* a notable feature of some processes of development and, moreover, to bring it about is often an important aim of practice. The importance of the conception of negation of negation lies in what it says about the conditions for such repetition. If features of an earlier stage are to be repeated at a later stage, that cannot take place by a simple return to the earlier stage—for that stage is past and cannot come back. It can only take place by their being reproduced at a later stage, in which case they are inevitably changed and modified in accordance with the character of that later stage. Thus features of the past can reappear in the future only as changed and transformed by the process of negation of negation and not by a simple return to the past.

This principle, like other principles of dialectics, has a quality of obviousness which is often overlooked. It is an obvious truth—but it is overlooked by all those who express a hankering to return to the past. Such hankerings must always be vain. It is in practice vitally important to realise that what is past *cannot* be restored when forward development is in operation. Nevertheless some features of the past may be restored, but only by carrying forward the process of development to a new stage, in which those features reappear in new ways—"on a higher level", as a negation of negation, enriched and transformed as a result of the first negation.

We have already seen how the negation of negation occurs in history in the development from primitive communism to communism. The second appearance of communism is only possible after going through the whole development of class-society—the first negation; and it embodies all that has been achieved during that development.

Again, in the history of thought, the "primitive, natural materialism" of the earliest philosophers was negated by philosophical idealism, and modern materialism arises only as the negation of that negation.

> "This modern materialism," wrote Engels in *Anti-Dühring*, "is not the mere re-establishment of the old, but adds to the permanent foundations of this old materialism the whole thought content of two thousand years of development of philosophy and natural science."

The practical importance of the negation of the negation can be seen most clearly if we take the example of the development of individual property, where it again occurs.

Marx, in the first volume of *Capital*, pointed out that the pre-capitalist "individual private property founded on the labours of the proprietor" is negated—destroyed—by capitalist private property. For capitalist private property arises only on the ruin and expropriation of the pre-capitalist individual producers. The individual producer used to own his instruments of production and his product—both were taken away from him by the capitalists. But when capitalist private property is itself negated—when "the expropriators are expropriated"—then the individual property of the producers is restored once more, but in a new form, on a higher level.

> "This does not re-establish private property for the producer, but gives him individual property based on the acquisitions of the capitalist era, i.e. on co-operation and the possession in common of the land and means of production."

The producer, as a participant in socialised production, then enjoys, as his individual property, a share of the social product—"according to his work" in the first stage of communist society, and "according to his needs" in the fully developed communist society.

When capitalism arose, the *only* way forward was through this negation of negation. Some of the British Chartists put forward in their land policy demands aimed at arresting the new capitalist process and restoring the *old* individual private property of the producer. This was vain. The only road forward for the producers was by the struggle against capitalism and for socialism—not to restore the *old* individual property which capitalism had destroyed, but to destroy capitalism and so re-create individual property on a *new*, socialist basis.

Similarly the Russian Narodniki, against whom Lenin fought in the 1890s, wanted somehow to arrest the process of capitalist development and restore the old peasant communes. Lenin's fight against them was based on showing that this was impossible.

The principle of negation of negation is thus an expression of the simple truth that one cannot put the clock back and reconstitute the past. One can only move forward into the future through the working out of all the contradictions contained within the given stage of development and through the negations consequent on them.

119

Chapter Eleven

A SCIENTIFIC WORLD OUTLOOK

Science and Materialism

Dialectical materialism, the philosophy adopted by Marxist parties, is a truly scientific world outlook. For it is based on considering things as they are, without arbitrary, pre-conceived assumptions (idealist fantasies); it insists that our conceptions of things must be based on actual investigation and experience, and must be constantly tested and re-tested in the light of practice and further experience.

Indeed, "dialectical materialism" means: understanding things just as they are ("materialism"), in their actual inter-connection and movement ("dialectics").

The same cannot be said about other philosophies. They all make arbitrary assumptions of one kind or another, and try to erect a "system" on the basis of those assumptions. But such assumptions are arbitrary only in appearance; in fact they express the various prejudices and illusions of definite classes.

Dialectical materialism is in no sense a philosophy "above science".

Others have set philosophy "above science", in the sense that they have thought they could discover what the world was like just by thinking about it, without relying on the data of the sciences, on practice and experience. And then, from this lofty standpoint, they have tried to dictate to the scientists, to tell them where they were wrong, what their discoveries "really meant" and so on.

But Marxism makes an end of the old philosophy which claimed to stand above science and to explain "the world as a whole".

"Modern materialism . . . no longer needs any philosophy standing above the sciences," wrote Engels in *Anti-Dühring*. "As soon as each separate science is required to get clarity as to its position in the great totality of things and of our knowledge of things a special science dealing with this totality is superfluous."

Dialectical materialism, he further wrote:

"is in fact no longer a philosophy, but a simple conception of the world which has to establish its validity and be applied not in a science of sciences standing apart, but within the positive sciences. . . . Philosophy is therefore . . . both abolished and preserved; abolished as regards its form, and preserved as regards its real content."

Our picture of the world about us, of nature, of natural objects and processes, their interconnections and laws of motion, is not to be derived from philosophical speculation, but from the investigations of the natural sciences.

The scientific picture of the world and its development is not complete, and never will be. But it has advanced far enough for us to realise that philosophical speculation is superfluous. And we should refuse to fill in gaps in scientific knowledge by speculation.

The growing picture of the world which natural science unfolds is a materialist picture—despite the many efforts of philosophers to make out the contrary. For step by step as science advances it shows how the rich variety of things and processes and changes to be found in the real world can be explained and understood in terms of material causes, without bringing in God or spirit or any supernatural agency.

Every advance of science is an advance of materialism against idealism, a conquest for materialism—although when driven out of one position idealism has always taken up another position and manifested itself again in new forms, so that in the past the sciences have never been consistently materialist.

For every advance of science means showing the order and development of the material world "from the material world itself".

Science and Socialism

The scientific character of Marxism is manifested especially in this, that it makes *socialism* into a science.

We do not base our socialism, as the utopians did, on a conception of abstract human nature. The utopians worked out schemes for an ideal society, but could not show how to achieve socialism in practice. Marxism made socialism into a science by basing it on an analysis of the actual movement of history, of the economic law of motion of capitalist society in particular, thus showing how socialism arises as the necessary next stage in the evolution of society, and how it can come about only by the waging of the working-class struggle, through the defeat of the capitalist class and the institution of the dictatorship of the proletariat.

Thus Marxism treats man himself, society and history, scientifically.

> "Socialism, since it has become a science, demands that it be pursued as a science," wrote Engels in his *Prefatory Note to "Peasant War in Germany"*, "that is, that it be studied. The task will be to spread with increased zeal among the masses of the workers the ever more clarified understanding thus acquired, to knit together ever more firmly the organisation both of the party and of the trade unions."

Scientific study of society shows that human history develops from stage to stage according to definite laws. Men themselves are the active force in this development. By understanding the laws of development of society, therefore, we can guide our own struggles and create our own socialist future.

Thus scientific socialism is the greatest and most important of all the sciences.

The practitioners of the natural sciences have been getting

worried because they feel that governments do not know how to put their discoveries to proper use. They have good cause to worry about this. Science is discovering the secrets of nuclear energy, for example; but its discoveries are being used to create weapons of destruction. Many people are even coming to believe that it would be better if we had no science, since its discoveries open up such terrifying possibilities of disaster.

How can we ensure that the discoveries of science are put to proper use for the benefit of mankind? It is scientific socialism alone which answers this problem. It teaches us what are the forces which make history and thereby shows us how we can make our own history today, change society and determine our own future. It teaches us, therefore, how to develop the sciences in the service of mankind, how to carry them forward in today's crisis. Physics can teach us how to release nuclear energy, it cannot teach us how to control the social use of that energy. For this there is required, not the science of the atom, but the science of society.

Conclusions

We have now briefly surveyed the principal features of the Marxist materialist conception of the world and of the Marxist dialectical method. What conclusions can we draw at this stage?

(1) The world outlook of dialectical materialism is a consistent and reasoned outlook, which derives its strength from the fact that it arises directly from the attempt to solve the outstanding problems of our time.

The epoch of capitalism is an epoch of stormy development in society. It is marked by revolutionary advances of the forces of production and of scientific discovery, and by consequent uninterrupted disturbance of all social conditions. This sets one theoretical task above all, and that is to arrive at an adequate conception of the laws of change and development in nature and society.

To this theoretical task dialectical materialism addresses itself.

(2) This is not the task of working out a philosophical

system, in the old sense. What is required is not any system of ideas spun out of the heads of philosophers, which we can then admire and contemplate as a system of "absolute truth".

Capitalist society is a society rent with contradictions, and the more it has developed the more menacing and intolerable for the working people have the consequences of these contradictions become. The new powers of production are not utilised for the benefit of society as a whole but for the profit of an exploiting minority. Instead of leading to universal plenty, the growth of the powers of production leads to recurrent economic crises, to unemployment, to poverty and to hideously destructive wars.

Therefore the philosophical problem of arriving at a true conception of the laws of change and development in nature and society becomes, for the working people, a practical political problem of finding how to change society, so that the vast new forces of production can be used in the service of humanity. For the first time in history the possibility of a full and rich life for everyone exists. The task is to find how to make that possibility a reality.

It is to the solution of this practical task that the theory of dialectical materialism is devoted.

(3) Addressing itself to this task, dialectical materialism is and can only be a partisan philosophy, the philosophy of a party, namely, of the party of the working class, whose object is to lead the millions of working people to the socialist revolution and the building of communist society.

(4) Dialectical materialism cannot but stand out in sharp contrast to the various contemporary schools of bourgeois philosophy.

What have these various schools of philosophy to offer at the present time? Systems and arguments by the bucketful— most of them neither original nor cogent, if one takes the trouble to analyse them closely. But no solution to the problems pressing upon the people of the capitalist countries and the colonies. How to end poverty? How to end war? How to utilise production for the benefit of all? How to end the oppression of one nation by another? How to end the exploitation of man by man? How to establish the brotherhood of men? These are our problems. We must judge philosophies by whether or not they show how to solve them. By that criterion, the philosophical schools of capitalism must one and all be judged—"weighed in the balance and found wanting".

The prevailing bourgeois philosophies, with all their differences, have in common a retreat from the great positive ideas which inspired progressive movements in the past. True, there remain within the ranks of bourgeois philosophy those who continue, according to their lights, trying to preserve and carry forward some of these positive ideas. For they are ideas which cannot by any manner of means be extinguished. But the prevailing philosophies emphasize men's helplessness and limitations; they speak of a mysterious universe; and they counsel either trust in God or else hopeless resignation to fate or blind chance. Why is this? It is because all these philosophies are rooted in acceptance of capitalism and cannot see beyond capitalism. From start to finish they reflect the insoluble crisis of the capitalist world.

(5) Dialectical materialism asks to be judged and will be judged by whether it serves as an effective instrument to show the way out of capitalist crisis and war, to show the way for the working people to win and wield political power, to show the way to build a socialist society in which there is no more exploitation of man by man and in which men win increasing mastery over nature.

Dialectical materialism is a philosophy of practice, indissolubly united with the practice of the struggle for socialism.

It is the philosophy born out of the great movement of our times—the movement of the people who labour, who "create all the good things of life and feed and clothe the world", to rise at last to their full stature. It is wholly, entirely dedicated to the service of that movement. This is the source of all its teachings, and in that service its conclusions are continually tried, tested and developed. Without such a philosophy, the movement cannot achieve consciousness of itself and of its tasks, cannot achieve unity, cannot win its battles.

Since the greatest task facing us is that of ending capitalist society and building socialism, it follows that the chief problem to which dialectical materialism addresses itself, and on the solution of which the whole philosophy of dialectical materialism turns, is the problem of understanding the forces of development of society. The chief problem is to reach such an understanding of society, of men's social activity and of the development of human consciousness, as will show us how to achieve and build the new socialist society and the new socialist consciousness. The materialist conception and dialectical method with which we have been concerned in this volume are applied to this task in the materialist conception of history.

READING LIST

The following are the principal works by Marx, Engels and Lenin setting forth general principles of the philosophy of dialectical materialism. The three marked with an asterisk are the best for beginners.

MARX AND ENGELS:
  The German Ideology, Part I

ENGELS:
  Socialism, Utopian and Scientific*
  Ludwig Feuerbach*
  Anti-Dühring
  The Dialectics of Nature

LENIN:
  The Teachings of Karl Marx*
  Materialism and Empirio-Criticism
  Philosophical Notebooks